Praise for **The Elepha.** ﹥m:

"Edgar Papke's *The Elephant in the Boardroom* provides a well-thought-out discussion of what leaders often forget: leading with intention. I found myself reading the book and asking if I led my own company in a manner that affords managers the opportunity to contribute to our success. In Chapter 7, "Loving Elephants," I love the idea that "You walk into the meeting room and ask the members of your team to help you identify all the conflicts that need to be talked about and are currently not being confronted." The book validates that leaders don't have all the answers or know what needs to be done next. It challenges you to walk with the elephants and positively address any conflicts that may be hindering growth."

—Heidi Gerding, CEO, HeiTech Services, Inc.

"*The Elephant in the Boardroom* absolutely captures Edgar Papke's essence as a student and teacher of business. He knows how to take a very deep-seated problem embedded in our business culture and dig it out for us to look at in a scientific and productive manner. He differentiates managing conflict from getting involved in conflict and clearly defines the emotional connection to conflict that is the usual suspect in preventing leaders from dealing with it. Deep inside, we think we need to do battle with others on their level, using their weapons, methods and rules of engagement. Edgar gives us tools to manage the interaction on our level, with our methods, and our rules of engagement."

—Dan Berman, CEO, PharmaCentra

"Benjamin Franklin stated, "In this world nothing can be said to be certain, except death and taxes." In *The Elephant in the Boardroom*, Edgar Papke does an extraordinary job of analyzing and discussing a third certainty for all leaders—conflict. As Papke poignantly points out, if it wasn't for conflict, leaders wouldn't exist. Papke freshly explores and navigates through the dysfunctions and dire consequences of avoiding conflict, as well as the steps and processes involved in embracing conflict, including its critical benefits. Papke demonstrates that embracing conflict is perhaps the single-most important skill you can develop in becoming a successful leader."

—Bob Pruitt, president, Cal-Tex Protective Coatings, Inc.

"A masterpiece.... *The Elephant in the Boardroom* goes way beyond the boardroom of any business and reaches anyone who wants a better relationship with their spouse, kids, parents, employees, bosses, or customers. This book builds on Edgar's brilliant book *True Alignment*, which helped me actively build our business's culture so we confront and face conflict rather than wait for the elephant to sit on us. Building such a culture is really hard to do, and having a framework and a starting point that both of these books provide is an imperative first step to building lasting authentic relationships."

—Ted Risdall, CEO, The Risdall Marketing Group

"Aligning a global culture to a shared purpose to differentiate and win is a tall task. Operating in 25 different countries to achieve this requires developing competencies in having deeper conversations that foster mutual understanding for superior execution. This is paramount to our ability to win. *The Elephant in the Boardroom* clearly articulates how embracing and managing conflict is a competency of communication we must grasp, practice, and apply. And, more importantly, that avoiding conflict is a true driver of dysfunction none of us can afford. Edgar provides excellent insights and useful tools that I put to work right away."

—Ralph J. Vasami, Chief Executive Officer,
Universal Weather and Aviation, Inc.

"With his new book, Edgar Papke brings the role of conflict into the forefront and examines how it impacts leaders on a daily basis. By framing conflict as an integral factor in becoming a great leader, he invites us to explore our own hesitations in dealing with it head-on and provides the necessary tools to do just that, and to become better leaders. I am especially encouraged by the fact that it is never too late to address our own legacies and that we each have the power within us to initiate change. The concept of 'fearless exploration' provides a definition of what we should all strive to achieve. I highly recommend this book to anyone looking to become a stronger leader."

—Lisa Rissetto, CEO, G. Hensler & Co.

"I love the premise and totally agree with the idea that it is impossible to understand how we manage conflict without knowing that 'our story' is sitting on our shoulders and running the show. I am a huge fan of *The Elephant in the Boardroom* and the approach of Leading With Intention, asking the question, 'What game am I really out to win? I'm also coming to understand that where intention was once an outcome, I now find that it is more of a journey that gets more refined with experience. I am thankful for Edgar Papke's commitment to put into words those ideas that matter most."

—Donald Myers, Vistage Chair

"I have experienced leadership as a great quest. When I was younger, I thought there were correct answers to every situation. I wanted the methodology to follow to get assured success. After 30 years as a manager, I am more intrigued by the authentic journey. In his book *The Elephant in the Boardroom*, Papke gives us his heartfelt, thoughtful framework and guide, reflecting his years of experience. Whether one is just starting out, or one is focused on developing new leaders at the end of a career, this book can help any leader."

—Chuck Peters, president and CEO, The Gazette Company

"A masterful work full of practical advice on how we expect leaders to face the great challenges and problems of our time (hint: courage is mentioned more than a few times). *The Elephant in the Boardroom* presents a clear roadmap for leaders to use breakdowns for breakthroughs to reach new levels of organizational effectiveness."

—Jan Rutherford, founder, Self-Reliant Leadership,
and author, *The Littlest Green Beret*

"In one book, Edgar Papke shows how a company and its leadership team can use constructive conflict as a path to innovation, entrepreneurship, and growth. *The Elephant in the Boardroom* gives us a simple and practical roadmap to how to accelerate success within business, regardless of size or industry. Our founder, my dad, built our company on the pillars of positive conflict. He would have been so impressed with Edgar and the logical approach to the many lessons in his new book. I plan on making it must-reading for our management team."

—Joseph Armentano, Chief Executive Officer, Paraco Gas Corp

"I grew up in a family that had elephants embedded in our lives. I started a company and unknowingly injected elephants into the relationships of my team. After reading this exceptional book, I understand the value of conflict and how confronting it generates creativity and demonstrates courage. Now, I am on a new path as a leader in search of elephants and for opportunities to identify conflict."

—Richard Yukes, president, Black Bear Oil Corp

"*The Elephant in the Boardroom* is a compelling new way for leaders to think about conflict and their relationship to it. Papke is a curator. He distills a complex conversation into the three core expectations we have about leadership. Leaders at every level will be well-served using his ideas to drive success and change."

—Joe Farlow Clark, CEO, Prana Business LLC

THE
ELEPHANT
IN THE
BOARDROOM

THE
ELEPHANT
IN THE
BOARDROOM

How Leaders Use and Manage Conflict
to Achieve Greater Levels of Success

EDGAR PAPKE

CAREER
PRESS
Pompton Plains, N.J.

THE ELEPHANT IN THE BOARDROOM
TYPESET BY KARA KUMPEL
Cover design by Ty Nowicki
Printed in the U.S.A.

To order this title, please call toll-free 1-800-CAREER-1 (NJ and Canada: 201-848-0310) to order using VISA or MasterCard, or for further information on books from Career Press.

The Career Press, Inc.
12 Parish Drive
Wayne, NJ 07470
www.careerpress.com

Library of Congress Cataloging-in-Publication Data
Papke, Edgar.
The elephant in the boardroom : how leaders use and manage conflict to reach greater levels of success / Edgar Papke. -- 1
        pages cm
Includes bibliographical references and index.
ISBN 978-1-63265-015-3 (paperback) -- ISBN 978-1-63265-983-5 (ebook) 1. Leadership. 2. Conflict management. 3. Success in business. I. Title.
HD57.7.P3637 2015
658.4'092--dc23
                                    2015028935

To Taylor, Trevor, Teagan, and Turner...I am ever so proud of your contribution to making this a better world for everyone you touch. To my grandchildren Cardyn, Judah, and Meyer...my hope is that this book contributes to a bright future, free of fear, and full of promise and love. To Lori, thank you for your unwavering love.

ACKNOWLEDGMENTS

My thanks go first to the most important people in my life, the members of my family. They not only encourage and support me in my constant curiosity and desire to explore the world around me, they also give me the never-ending love that nourishes my being—my heart and soul.

Thank you to Theresa Blanding for being a wonderful and trusted sounding board and business companion, and for challenging and critiquing my many thoughts and ideas that resulted from my experiences, observations, and imagination. It's been almost a decade since we met and I couldn't ask for a better friend to share my journey on the path of studying and teaching the human art of business.

Thank you to Maryann Karinch. Every author should be as fortunate as I am to have such a wonderful and committed literary agent. Her candid guidance and advice is of tremendous value. Her integrity is unquestionable and her dedication unsurpassed.

Thank you to the many friends and colleagues that have contributed their feedback and insights during the past quarter of a century. My conversations with the many experts who have generously shared their experiences are invaluable and keep me challenged.

Thank you to the extraordinary number of CEOs, executives, and business and community leaders that I have had the pleasure to work with. This includes the over 19,000 Vistage and TEC members that have let me share my ideas and generously offered feedback on the application and value of my work.

Finally, to my clients, I am forever grateful for all the intimate and meaningful conversations that we have shared. You allow me to be a part of your lives in a way that makes me feel extremely privileged and honored. I am thankful for your trust, your confidence, and for your commitment to exploring the possibilities the world has to offer. I am forever grateful for your contributions and intention toward creating a promising future for the generations that follow you.

CONTENTS

INTRODUCTION

If you are a leader, or aspire to become one, this book is for you. It is intended for anyone in a leadership role, those wanting to become a leader, or anyone interested in the current state of leadership. This includes leaders at all levels of our organizations and communities, students and scholars, those in public service, and anyone interested in taking a leadership role—regardless of when and where.

This book is also about you. It is about how you embrace the responsibility to accept and deliver on the most demanding aspect of becoming and being a great leader: using and managing conflict to create positive change. Virtually everything you are expected to do to be successful as a leader originates from or is in some way connected to conflict. It is why understanding your unique relationship to conflict is the single most important aspect of your ability to lead. And, if you are like most leaders, you are probably struggling with it.

The intention of this book is to provide you with insight into the unique and powerful bond between conflict and who you are as a leader. It is the ultimate test that you, as a leader, face. Regardless of which approach to leadership you may subscribe to, the primary challenge to becoming a great leader is to confront and constructively manage the conflict that is at the heart of how our institutions, organizations, and teams function; conflict that is the result of the innate desire of human beings to compete and fulfill our wants and needs, and that reveals our differing views, values, beliefs, and ideas; conflict that also too easily manifests into dysfunctional, unproductive, and destructive behavior.

Great leadership begins with recognizing and exploring the intimate bond between leadership and conflict, and the trait that separates great leaders from all the others. It is at the core of your journey to becoming a great leader. This first step is not an easy one. In fact, in a survey of more than 4,000 leaders that included CEOs, executives, and managers, more than 90 percent admitted they were uncomfortable with confronting or engaging in conflict. They express clearly that they "do not like confronting conflict." In connection to these results, recent studies and surveys by a number of well-respected business schools, including Stanford and Harvard Universities, confirm what leadership and organizational experts, scholars, consultants, and coaches have recognized for decades. The top reason leaders and executives seek coaching is to manage conflict more effectively and make better and more focused strategic decisions.[1] These two challenges are actually one and the same. After all, strategy is the means through which we organize and venture to compete. Whether this strategy emerges through leading change, building teams, mentoring talent, strategic decision-making, developing and leading an organization's culture, or winning in the marketplace, it is always about conflict.

To be a truly successful leader requires you to be aware and operate at four levels: global, organizational, interpersonal, and self. Each level presents its own set of challenges. At the global level, you need to be aware of worldwide environmental, economic, and social forces and trends. Along with new emerging economies are the technologies and accompanying forms of social context that create the canvas of global competition and conflict. In your day-to-day role you may not always be aware of your connection to the global level. Yet, everything you do will affect or contribute to the greater world. In fact, the more aware you are of this, the further you can consciously choose to create a larger imprint and contribute more broadly. Never underestimate what you, as a single committed person, can accomplish.

The organizational level requires you to be aware of what is happening in your businesses, communities, and institutions. In particular, this demands that you are conscious of how your organization operates. To be an astute student and leader, you must have an intimate knowledge of your institution's culture and how teamwork happens. Knowing the rules of engagement at the company and team level is key to contributing to the company's ability to compete and succeed in the marketplace, and to influence the relationships among its members to collaborate in pursuing a shared purpose and vision.

At the interpersonal level, your awareness will be key to effectively communicating with and motivating others. Being mindful and attentive to every person you engage with requires you to be aware of your emotions and actions. You must be conscious of the behaviors through which you create mutual respect, trust, and reciprocity. To be successful, you will need to constantly strive for self-awareness. For without it, you will not know how you connect with others on a personal level, let alone at the organizational and global levels.

So how do you begin to take on this challenge? It starts with better understanding and embracing the natural relationship of leadership and conflict, and learning to apply self-knowledge in effectively confronting and managing it. Repeatedly, my conversations with leaders are about the conflicts that inevitably get in the way of their success. Time and again, leaders share their disappointment in the lack of constructive conflict management and the resulting dysfunction that cripples their organizations and teams, and undermines their ability to lead effectively.

The conclusion is obvious: you must learn to confront the "elephant in the room." You must learn and develop the capability to find, root out, and manage the elephants living and thriving in your organization, team, or business. If you fail to willingly and effectively face conflict, you will eventually undermine your influence and the capability of your team and organization to perform.

The failure of leaders to confront and deal with conflict successfully is evident throughout our businesses, governments, and schools. Plagued by the inability of leaders to leverage the opportunities that conflict offers, a vast majority of our institutions, and our broader social realm, lack this critical component of leadership. As a result, the people and the organizations they serve do not perform at the levels they are capable of. The cultures of their organizations fail to develop in a healthy manner and the people in them never feel safe and empowered. Show me a leader that fails to confront conflict and I'll show you the biggest elephant in the room.

To be truly successful, leaders must stop avoiding and misusing conflict; rather, they should embrace it as the true source of influence and power that it is. They must learn to embrace the idea that confronting conflict is the positive leadership trait that most benefits their careers, reputations, and legacies. To succeed, you must understand that conflict is a source of critical and creative thinking that drives the innovation and change you are responsible and accountable for leading.

To do so effectively requires that you are conscious of the personal risks and fears that keep you from actively addressing the elephants in the room. It is necessary to develop the ability to address your own internal conflicts and not let them become your personal Achilles heel. In today's world, this includes the desire for celebrity that accompanies the role of being a successful leader; a celebrity resulting from the ever-increasing and real-time feedback of the expanding media that naturally feeds one's ego. More than ever, it is important to avoid falling into the unsettling energy that is pervasive in the environments you are operating in.

We are undergoing a shift in how the world operates. We have created a world with virtually no boundaries on the access to and sharing of information and knowledge. The question is: Where are we heading next? From the industrial age to the age of information and knowledge, we are undergoing another shift. This time, we are moving into the age of awareness. This is a time in human history when we must learn much more about who we are as human beings and how to make use of all the information and knowledge that is at our fingertips. It is a time in which we learn to rely less on technology that creates a world of impersonal connectivity to one that connects us to our humanity. It is about the quality of our relationships to one another as people participating in our shared human experience. It is about trust.

I realize I am not alone in seeing the world through this lens. For us to truly meet the many challenges we face now and will face in the future requires leadership that does not shy away from the host of conflicts we engage in. Rather, at all levels, we require that a more aware form of leadership emerges that confronts those conflicts in new and more productive ways. Throughout the organizations and institutions of our capitalistic democracies, we yearn for leadership that is more aware and focused on creating positive changes and solutions that benefits us all, leadership that confronts conflict in constructive ways.

The Elephant in the Boardroom will not provide you with all the solutions and answers to all the big problems and conflicts of our day. What I do intend is to offer you a set of insights and suggestions to help you better understand the unique relationship between leadership and conflict, to explore your own personal relationship to conflict, and provide some ideas and approaches to manage conflict in constructive ways. Conflict is the greatest asset of leaders, driving the innovation and creativity that we rely on for creating the future. Therefore, it is your greatest asset.

Throughout this book, I am inviting you to explore your personal relationship to conflict and to examine your values, beliefs, and personal motivations. To do so, you have to use the most powerful aspect of your leadership behavior, the power of choice. Using self-knowledge as a springboard to success, I invite you to understand the personal responsibility you have to your team and organization, and identify where you can improve. Doing so will also help you manage conflict in all aspects of your life. In the end, at both a professional and personal level, your success depends on your ability to confront and manage conflict effectively, and to use it to develop mutually respectful and beneficial relationships.

This book is presented in three interdependent sections. Part One focuses on the unique relationship that exists between leaders and conflict. It provides you with insight into the natural aspects of this relationship and the need to embrace it as a key to lead effectively. It explores how leaders develop and lead cultures that thrive on conflict to drive innovation and higher levels of performance.

Part Two invites you to explore your life story, your intimate relationship to conflict, and your self-concept. At the core of your personal experiences are the values and beliefs that act as the sources of your emotional responses and resulting behaviors. Knowing your self enables you to leverage your self-concept to manifest your power to choose how to confront and use conflict to perform at higher levels of leadership.

Part Three focuses on leading with intention, providing a seven-step model for effectively managing conflict and moving toward productive problem solving and mutually benefitting resolutions. My hope is that you are able to use some of the tools and techniques this section of the book offers you. By bringing together the framework for leading with intention with the key aspects of the book's first two parts, my goal is to lead you through a learning process focusing on how to face conflict and, with authenticity and confidence, confront it effectively so that you can use and manage it to reach greater levels of success.

The world is yearning for great leadership. It is time for you to make your contribution to it. Thank you for allowing me to be part of your journey.

Edgar Papke

Louisville, Colorado

May 2015

Part I

LEADERS AND CONFLICT:
A UNIQUE RELATIONSHIP, AN INTIMATE BOND

Chapter 1

WHAT WE EXPECT OF GREAT LEADERS

The world we have created continues to evolve at an increasing pace. During the past century, the psychological effect of the spiraling rate of change on virtually every human being is dizzying. As we speed toward a future full of increasingly difficult challenges, the result is a world that continues to become more complex.

In order to keep pace with this increased complexity, we have created more intricate and demanding expectations for leaders. We have not only set the bar higher for leaders to be successful, but we have also created myriad complex hoops for them to jump through.

During the past several decades, the study of leadership has continued to expand. Our definition of great leadership has taken on a broadening set of competencies, ideas, values, performance demands, and expectations for accountability. It leaves one wondering: What school of thought, form of influence, or characteristics and traits does a leader need to be successful?

Such circumstances can make effective leadership a grim proposition. It creates a definition of success so confusing that it keeps potentially good—and especially great—leaders from emerging, leaders the world is yearning for. It is as if society has shaped a context and set of conditions in which individuals avoid the responsibility to lead. This includes individuals in business organizations, governments, and institutions of learning.

When I ask people to identify what great leaders do, I always expect to get a wide range of responses. Great leaders:

- Create and communicate a vision.
- Define the mission.
- Articulate purpose.
- Hold others accountable.
- Make great decisions.
- Collaborate.
- Take the right risks.
- Need to be lifelong learners.
- Are always aligned with their values and beliefs.
- Successfully coach others.
- Challenge themselves and others.
- Strive for continuous improvement.
- Build great teams.
- Ask the right questions.
- Drive innovation.
- Lead by example.
- Set clear expectations.

You get the point. And as you can imagine, the list goes on. I'm sure you can add a few I have not mentioned. These expectations are hard to argue against; they are all valid examples of what leaders do to succeed.

Eventually, the expectations of what success looks like gets into some seriously challenging territory, often resulting in demands virtually impossible for any human being to meet. These demands include talents and virtues such as seeing into the future, having an answer to every problem, anticipating the next great trend, not making mistakes, always saying the right thing, keeping every commitment, always being truthful, and having the thick skin of a rhino.

In the end, it's clear that the long list of expectations we hold for leaders creates a daunting task. Whether provided by the scholars of leadership, the armchair blogging experts with lists such as "10 Amazing Things," "15 Essential Skills," "23 Qualities," "9 Pursuits," "12 Habits," and "101 Things Great Leaders Do," or the formulas and approaches prescribed by the thousands of leadership development courses and coaching programs, it's no wonder that most of today's leaders are willing to try just about anything to succeed. It is big business, with everyone that has anything to say about leadership jumping into the fray and playing the market to sell their version of the secret sauce, the hidden gems, or a new and bold paradigm of leadership.

The result is that anyone paying attention to it all and trying just a fraction of the available solutions winds up pursuing a hit-and-miss approach that is confusing, unfocused, and inconsistent. It also causes them to jump from one approach or popular fad to another. Ultimately, it's a minefield so fraught with the possibility of failure that leaders turn to playing it safe, not taking risks, and avoiding the more difficult issues and challenges we face.

As much as organizations undertake fads in leadership development, why have they failed to take hold? The fact is that the expectations are so broad and confusing, that most people who undertake leadership roles eventually lose their motivation to lead. Or they succumb to holding on to their position, fearful of doing things differently and risk losing it. They are afraid of failing because it has become so easy to fail.

As we look to the future, it is important to regain a perspective of leadership that engages potential future leaders and offers a clear path to success. For the past 25 years, I have had the good fortune of spending most of my time studying and exploring leadership and working with and coaching leaders. As a result, I've concluded that all the activities leaders engage in—every pursuit, action, and interaction—ultimately result in three expectations we have of great leaders. It is with these expectations that we now begin exploring the role of conflict in leadership.

The Three Expectations

In complexity, lives simplicity.

Above all else, we expect great leaders to do three things successfully: 1) create change; 2) confront conflict; and 3) strive for self-knowledge. If this sounds simplistic, I suggest you go through the long lists and offerings of what great leaders do and sort them into these three distinct core expectations. You'll find that virtually all of the things leaders do contribute to these three pursuits. The three are interdependent and, therefore, have equal value and importance.

Creating Change

A good place to start is exploring and understanding expectations of creating change. There are several good reasons to believe that the origins of leadership came from the desire of human beings for control and, on their own terms, manifesting change. It is also important to recognize that the desire to create change results from the need to confront conflict, which itself comes from the tension created by the gap between what we have and what we want. We look to leaders to address this gap and show us the path to resolving it.

When a situation arises for the need for change and action, the first person to act typically takes on the leadership role. For example: A group of people is confronted with an unwanted circumstance and an action or intervention is needed. For some reason, they want something to change. It might simply be that they are dissatisfied with what they have and want more. Or, they are in some way threatened and there is a condition that requires a response. The first person to act, to step up and engage others in taking action to creating a resolution, becomes the de facto leader. For lack of a better analogy, the person is filling a leadership vacuum. And if the action he or she takes and leads others to undertake succeeds, it further establishes their leadership influence.

This is an undeniable aspect of the phenomenon of leadership. Those that can create change are looked to as leaders. When they do it on a grander scale, they become our heroes. Like Martin Luther King, Mahatma Gandhi, John F. Kennedy, Rosa Parks, Henry Ford, and Bill Gates, their names are reminders of what is possible, how we can attain a brighter future, how we can overcome the forces that keep us from moving ahead, and how we can fulfill our deepest desires and needs. They are the shining lights of leadership. They are the individuals willing to step out and take the risk to confront a situation and create change. When a leader does so successfully, he or she gets the added benefit of trust from those who are willing to follow. The truth is that we all want change; we just long to have a sense of control over it. As human beings, we are naturally engaged in the quest for the mastery of change. To verify this, all one has to do is look at the accelerating rate of change we are engaged in and the realization of human potential that results in the extraordinary levels of creativity and innovation. Many leaders of organizations and companies speak the language of innovation and improvement. What they are actually talking about is creating change.

Articulating and communicating a vision, defining a mission or purpose, taking a new or radical approach, and showing others a path to success are all activities and elements of creating change. Being creative and innovative, seeking solutions to our biggest social and business problems, and collaborating and forming partnerships with others are all a part of fulfilling the expectation of creating change. Having a strategy is simply having a plan for change.

We are never satisfied. When a leader successfully leads us to accomplish the change we seek, the next questions we ask are, "What's next?" and "What else can you do for us?" We have an ever present and unsatisfied hunger for change. It is what moves us forward in life and keeps our world advancing. What we often overlook is that our desire for change is the result of conflict. This conflict is the expression of the natural tension that comes from the gap between what we have and what we long for. The result of that conflict is the expectation that a leader will emerge and confront it, thereby leading us to create the change needed to manifest a resolution that meets our needs.

The ability of a leader to create positive change requires not only clearly articulating and consistently communicating a vision of the future state, but also emotionally engaging others, connecting them to the needs that motivate them. In order to do this effectively, you must have the trust of others. To do so successfully most often requires that you undertake the challenge to change your own way of how you do things. As a leader, you must be willing to change, grow, and evolve.

As everything in our world is changing and we look to leaders to guide us, why do we so often see leaders not willing to change themselves? Is this why so many of our institutions are lacking leadership? To expect others to engage in change and truly alter how things get done requires that you role model and reinforce the ability to change yourself. New habits in how you role model change will require new behaviors. This includes changes in how you engage with and influence others.

Confronting Conflict

When we create change, we invite and confront conflict. The interdependence of change and conflict is one of the great forces and natural tensions of human behavior. Yet, we often don't realize this relationship. I find that even among leaders, this relationship is often overlooked until they realize that they experience it all the time. It is a constant state that leaders live in.

Conflict and the desire for change are what bring us together. The energy of the relationship between conflict and change is also what tears us apart. It is through this dynamic tension that the need to confront conflict emerges. Yet, all too often leaders avoid doing so. This is problematic and lies at the center of the failure of so many leaders to effectively manage the many conflicts they face. Most leaders will say that they are uncomfortable with conflict and do not like to confront it.

Each year, through workshops, presentations, and coaching, I have the privilege of working and interacting with more than 1,000 Chief Executives, business leaders, and community leaders. Often, our conversations bring us to a place of significant intimacy. Regardless of where the conversation starts, the vast majority of time our dialogues end up being about conflict. More often than not, we focus on avoidance and the difficulty to confront conflict. I then ask, why as leaders, they do not confront conflict? What I have learned is that the dislike of conflict and confrontation among leaders stems from three key reasons: 1) the fear of being or appearing incompetent and failing; 2) the fear of being disliked; and 3) the absence of a perspective and belief that confronting conflict presents them with opportunity.

The first of these, the fear of being or appearing incompetent, is the one that keeps most leaders from constructively confronting conflict. It begins with the notion that leaders are supposed to get it right, have the answers, be the smartest person in the room, and know the right things to do. I have observed that for leaders, it is not always just about being right; it is often about being competent in getting there. Unfortunately, most leaders are not given the opportunity to learn about conflict at a level that develops the competencies, skills, and know-how they need to be effective.

Few leaders receive training and development in conflict management. Those who do, however, typically attend a day or two of training and do not receive the benefit of ongoing coaching, guidance, and feedback on how to apply their learning. Without sustained development, it is no wonder they don't undergo noticeable or sustained improvement. Most leaders learn how to manage conflict through trial and error. Even more doomed are the leaders that experience only the aggressive aspects of conflict and, because they are always busy winning and satisfying themselves, never learn to collaborate and engage in shared problem solving with others.

The consequences of appearing incompetent include feeling stupid, inept, and incapable. Leaders often tell me that when it comes to confronting conflict, they "feel like a failure." Underlying this are feelings of embarrassment, humiliation, and shame that results from thinking you are not good enough. The fear of appearing incompetent is a powerful reason for leaders to avoid conflict. And whereas leaders often state that they ignore conflicts in their organizations because they are not worth their time, are not important enough, or are without value, when we look deeper we typically find that the fear of not being competent to manage conflict is the root cause. It is easy to ignore something that is laden with potentially negative consequences. Unfortunately, in the absence of competency, leaders will usually fall back on the "my way or the highway" approach. After all, when you don't have another option, you often turn to what you believe is the proven course of action and one you're most familiar with.

The notion that a conflict is not worth your time is often deceiving. In most cases, what does not appear important enough to engage in now will more than likely require your attention later. When it does, it will likely take more time and attention than if you had confronted it the first time. Frequently, a conflict ignored will present itself again. The consequence of this procrastination is that the conflict has had time to further develop and fester. The same conflict will then likely appear as a more difficult problem and will have stronger emotional attachments.

The second most frequent response as to why leaders do not like conflict is fear of not being liked. This fear is a very powerful force. We all want to be liked and loved. Not only do leaders want to be liked and loved, they also want to be admired for who they are and what they represent. The idea that their values and beliefs are to be revered and respected by others gives value to the leader and his or her self-concept. It is an all too often accepted fallacy that a leader need not be liked, only respected. To some degree, we all want to be liked, loved, and accepted by others. It is human.

Being liked influences one's ability and desire to be open and honest. For all of us, the idea of honestly confronting a conflict is fraught with the risk of being personally rejected. In simple terms, if I am honest with you and confront a difference we have, you may reject or not like me for it. And whereas vulnerability may put one at risk of appearing incompetent, the greater risk is that others will not like us because we told them something they didn't want to hear. As we'll explore further in Part Three, the fear of rejection for sharing one's truth influences how honestly we can confront one another and whether we choose to withhold our truth or openly express it.

The third source of avoiding conflict is the perceived absence of opportunity. More often than not, leaders say things such as, "there's nothing in it for me" or "it's not worth my time." This perspective is a big mistake and has multiple consequences including missed opportunities to challenge themselves and others to think more critically. This results in the failure to acknowledge how confronting conflict will benefit others, the team, and the organization.

Avoiding conflict results in constraints to innovation and creativity. Because the leader takes the path of least resistance, so do the people he or she leads. Furthermore, avoiding conflict often results in the suppression of dissent and constructive critical thinking. It can also easily lead to compliance, obedience, and false compromise. Leadership is challenging people to think critically and creatively to confront conflicts rather than compromising to maintain a status quo. Usually, the potential benefit is overlooked because of the perceived absence of opportunity. However, every conflict presents an opportunity. True leaders engage others in conflict, guiding them to find and understand the truth.

Other opportunities missed through avoiding conflict are those that more directly benefit the leader. These are often not on the leaders' radar screen, yet they convey the influences essential to their success. One of the most important of these is the influence of courage. The effect of your courage cannot be overstated. As a leader, you are expected to be brave and have the backbone to confront conflict and take on difficult challenges. Others assume that you will step into the fray and confront others that are in conflict with one another. It is the sign of great leadership and reflects the idea that we look for leaders to help us in our engagement with conflicts in our society, our institutions, and our lives. True leaders are not deterred by conflict. They see that within every conflict lies an opportunity. True leaders do not avoid conflict; they thrive on it.

Striving for Self-Knowledge

Behaviors are the expression of human emotion and therefore convey your wants, needs, and desires. Further, both your spoken words and your actions influence others. This idea forms the basis of the notion that to be truly successful as a leader requires you to continuously strive for self-knowledge and awareness of your emotions and behaviors. This means that you must go beyond just knowing and leveraging your competencies and skills. As a leader, you are expected to be a lifelong learner and strive for self-knowledge at deeper levels, requiring you to develop your social and emotional intelligence. Only then will you open up to the continual self-improvement and learning needed to become a great leader.

This is true for anyone who is on the path to becoming a leader. When it isn't, we find people in positions of leadership that are not truly equipped to successfully fill their roles. For as much as politicians are just politicians (and usually don't turn into real leaders), CEOs, executives, and managers also don't often become true leaders. They typically find themselves in leadership roles through merely displaying management skills and competencies and are unable to make the transition to leadership. And when they fail to become true leaders, they all too often take on the roles of the coalition builders. Or they become the keepers of conflict avoidance and the supporters of dysfunction by keeping themselves and others safe from criticism or challenges to their power.

The consequences of not striving for self-knowledge and making the transition to becoming a true leader are as negative as they are obvious. Through avoidance of conflict, a leader forms an inner circle that unfortunately also keeps potential leaders—those who may have the most positive effect—from reaching positions of leadership in organizations and institutions that need them most. There is a difference between wanting authority and taking responsibility. Too many times, people define leadership as only having a position of authority while leaving responsibility to others. Yielding responsibility, being compliant, and being unaccountable leads to complacency; it leads to a false sense of achievement that results in leaders and their teams or organizations without enough innovative and creative energy. The simple truth is that everyone lessens their expectations. Without striving for self-knowledge and making conscious and wise choices, these trappings are all too easy for potential leaders to fall into.

Striving for self-knowledge is critical to making the right choices. This is particularly true when it comes to understanding your self-concept and how to choose the behaviors that best align with your desired legacy. These behaviors include how to influence your relationships in the most positive and constructive ways. We expect leaders to know their strengths and weaknesses as they relate to their competencies and skills. We also expect them to know their interpersonal strengths and challenges and to have the wherewithal to make the right choices.

To be effective, you must understand your personal relationship to change. That requires having an intimate knowledge and understanding of your relationship to conflict. Without it, you will not be effective or be trusted to undertake the challenges that must be faced. Striving for self-knowledge is a trait and pursuit that no true leader can do without.

We expect leaders to demonstrate the qualities that most people strive for in their own lives. Humility, openness, vulnerability, responsibility, integrity, honesty, gratitude, compassion, the ability to listen, and respect for others—these are all qualities that we associate with a connectivity to humanity that we expect from great leaders. They are the sources of influence that we look for and admire in them. The truth is that without self-knowledge, it is difficult to imagine a person demonstrating the qualities that result from becoming more aware of his or her emotions, understanding the origins of those emotions, and leveraging the power to choose their behavior. True leaders are expected to choose wisely and, in the moment, take the most effective action.

Stepping Into Reality

The reality is that what separates effective leaders from ineffective ones is the ability to meet the three expectations of great leadership. True leaders also come to realize that without conflict, their roles and lives would likely feel empty. There would be no purpose and commitment to their existence and legacies. There comes a time when they find that conflict is the source of the need to lead. As a result, great leaders flourish when they embrace the unique relationship between leadership and conflict and see it not as a set of theories and abstract pursuits. Rather, as a lifelong quest for self-knowledge and understanding. Whereas others may be in it for the quick win, true leaders are in it for the long haul, recognizing that learning to use and manage conflict is the key to reaching greater levels of personal success and fulfillment of their legacies.

In today's world, this is not easy. The world is more complex than ever and we can only expect that it will continue to offer more complex challenges. The world is looking for new leaders who are willing to challenge the status quo and invite others to participate and contribute to confronting conflict in creative and constructive ways.

Unfortunately, the truth is that those striving to constructively confront conflict will always encounter others committed to resisting positive change. The latter maintain that conflict is best faced with overly aggressive and combative approaches and will want to keep things the way they are, regardless of how caustic and damaging the consequences are. They will avoid confronting difficult challenges and, thus, remain committed to maintaining dysfunction. These are the ineffective leaders who fail to grasp that avoidance of conflict eventually takes center stage. They are the biggest elephants.

True leaders, on the other hand, remain committed to constructively confronting conflict. They view it as a moral obligation of leadership to confront conflict and find constructive means through which to leverage it as opportunity, looking ahead with a clear line of sight to what is possible. They influence others to pursue a shared and mutually benefitting future. Like any other cause of conflict, the resistance and arrogance of others is a powerful source that summons a great leader's creativity, imagination, and resourcefulness. It feeds the fire and desire to seek the higher ground, the better way, the more productive use of disagreement, discourse, and differing ideas.

True leaders embrace their unique relationship to conflict. They come to recognize that leadership and conflict are continually converging. Great leaders embrace their undeniable bond to conflict and come to discover that they are one.

Chapter Summary

⟊ Our definition of great leadership has taken on an ever-broadening set of competencies, ideas, values, performance demands, and expectations for accountability.

⟊ There are three core expectations that we have of leaders: creating change, confronting conflict, and self-knowledge. The three are interdependent.

⟊ Creating change and conflict are virtually inseparable and together provide the engine for innovation.

⟊ Great leaders are those who thrive on conflict, recognizing it as opportunity.

⟊ Self-knowledge is critical to your ability to confront conflict and make good decisions.

⟊ Great leaders understand that conflict is the force that drives innovation and results in higher levels of success.

Chapter 2

LIVING YOUR LEGACY

As a leader, your legacy is defined by the quality of the relationships you have with everyone you touch. In a material sense, the reality is that we all come into the world with nothing and we leave with nothing. What you will leave behind is a legacy, a life's story that conveys the quality of your character and your influence on others.

It's Always About Relationships

There are many tales of leaders that are all too interested in their own outcomes of excessive wealth and power. One has to be careful. Despite material and power gains, your legacy will be determined more by how you used them to benefit others.

Realizing that your legacy will be defined by the quality of your relationships reminds you that you are connected to not only those who are close to you and with whom you interact daily, as

LIVING YOUR LEGACY

well as people you will never actually meet and who you will in-fluence from afar. In today's world of surface intimacy, how others see you can shift suddenly from moment to moment. For example, social media and wider access of information has heightened our ideals and broadened our view of good leadership and, therefore, has made it more difficult to become a great leader.

Your relationships and your level of success will be defined by the perceptions that others will form and invent about you. Their perceptions of you will be based on their observations and infer-ences of your behavior and actions, the decisions you make, the commitments they believe you are making, and the spectrum of unspoken expectations they have for you. These expectations in-clude how you live up to the standards of values, principles, and ethics that they presume you have. You are a human being just like they are. As a leader, though, you will be held to a higher standard, however unfair this may seem.

Another inescapable truth is that others will easily pin their hopes on you. As unfair as this may also sound, it is a charge of leadership that you must come to expect and accept. Whether it is employees expecting you to help them create the changes in their lives necessary to reach their goals and dreams, customers want-ing to fulfill their needs and wants, or taking the lead on signifi-cant social changes, everyone will have hope.

Always remember that people will respond or choose to follow you because you hold a position of influence and have the power of authority that comes with it. However, they will also respond to you based on your commitment to the greater service to others. These are attributes that allow others to see you for the true person you are, and also are acknowledgments of your self-concept, which convey the authenticity required to be a truly great leader.

As human beings, when we evaluate or judge the quality of our relationships, we interpret whether we are keeping the promises and commitments we make to one another. Without mutual benefit, we do not trust in the relationship. Leaders know the importance of keeping commitments. They take responsibility for making the promises and making sure they do everything in their power to deliver on them. The key to being trusted is keeping your commitments to the people you directly work and interact with, as well as those that are observing you from afar. As a leader, there is a ripple effect to every time you keep or don't keep a commitment. Many leaders are in it for the quick win and do not concern themselves with the longer term. Often, this can diminish and even undermine their legacies.

It is also true that there will be a disproportionate amount of attention paid to the times you fail to live up to your commitments. Your everyday success will have less influence and draw less attention than when you make mistake. This is a reality of leadership. It's also a good reason to face the truth when you do make a mistake. To avoid or try to conceal a mistake is inviting an elephant into the room. The humility that you convey in being honest and open about your own mistakes will gain you much more trust than trying to hide it, pass it off, or blame it on someone else.

The Slippery Slope of Unspoken Expectations

As a leader, the commitments you are responsible for are primarily the result of the expectations others will have of you. These expectations fall into two groups: those that are spoken and those that are unspoken. As an example of an unspoken expectation, it is expected by others that you will not withhold information from someone if it may keep the person from attaining a higher level of performance. Regardless of whether it is ever spoken or not, there is an expectation that, as leader, you will share that information. Regardless of how uncomfortable or difficult it may be, you will be meeting the unspoken expectation of transparency.

On the other hand, because it feels uncomfortable, you hold off sharing the information until it's too late. When asked about it later, you have the choice to admit that you knew or not. Or, you can rationalize your behavior as never having agreed to share such information. That is, because you had no prior agreement that it was your responsibility to share the information, you are not accountable for not having done so. In other words, it is an unspoken expectation and, because it was not spoken, you are not accountable.

The consequence of choosing not to take responsibility for failing to share the information may leave you feeling like you are in the right. And, because you made a good argument for not doing so, the other person should take accountability for not asking for or seeking the information. They will learn from the situation and know better next time. In other words, it was not a breakdown in leadership; rather, it was the other person's fault.

On the other hand, the person may feel that, as a leader, you did not perform at the level expected. As well, others who are aware of the situation and your actions may also decide that you failed to act in the manner that a person in your position should. This includes not only sharing the information you had, but also taking responsibility for not meeting their expectations.

Unspoken expectations are the slippery slopes to disappointment, resentment, and anger. We all hold expectations of one another. When they are met, all is well. When they go unmet, we are disappointed. And, because we feel in some way ignored, rejected, or taken advantage of, we get angry or feel resentment toward the person who is letting us down. In any relationship, when a mutual benefit we are expecting goes unmet, we blame the other person.

All too often, because we don't confront it when it happens, the unmet expectation never gets talked about and begins to fester in the relationship. This can lead to a variety of dysfunctional behaviors including "getting even."

Regardless of the relationship, it is hard to overstate the value of bringing unspoken expectations into the spoken realm. Above all, your longer-term success requires a commitment to meeting unspoken expectations such as honesty and always speaking your truth, regardless of how difficult it may be.

Trusting in the Truth

Always be careful and considerate in choosing your leadership path. Whether you are a CEO, manager, team leader, or in any other position, your legacy will reach beyond the people you have immediate interaction with. In doing so, you will have the opportunity to be authentic and openly express your dreams and aspirations. A great legacy conveys your heart and soul.

You must expect that sometimes your actions will result in deep emotional responses from others. Some of your actions will be well received by those aligned with your values and beliefs. There will also be those who will question your motives. They will criticize you for their perceptions of your values and beliefs, and disagree with your choices and actions. Their opinions of you are all stark reminders of the risk that you accept when you act in alignment to your values and beliefs, and express what you believe to be in the greater good. Needless to say, you will always feel like you're being tested. At certain times, the challenges you face will be much more difficult and you will need to find the courage to trust in and express your truth.

Too often we see leaders that try to sidestep or avoid sharing the truth. Yet, that's what most people crave. What makes leaders wary of being intimate and vulnerable are the fears of losing the trust of their followers and the power they represent. Whether because of appearing incompetent or being rejected for their values and beliefs, often leaders fear that the truth will threaten their leadership, that being vulnerable is a weakness they cannot afford to risk. This is not true. Vulnerability is a fear we all share, thus making it a powerful force of influence on others to participate in confronting difficult situations. As a leader, there is a time-tested adage that to get power, one has to give power. Truth is power. There is a natural reciprocity in the truth. As a leader, when you share the truth with others, most will feel trusted and will reciprocate by trusting you.

Being open and honest emotionally motivates others to contribute to finding and implementing solutions to even the most difficult challenges. It invites others to honestly express what they see, think, and feel. The result is an increased understanding of the problem at hand and an improved understanding of one another. A misstep too many leaders make is that they must have the answers and solutions. Vulnerability and sharing the truth will overcome the need to always be in control, be at the center, or to be liked and loved by everyone. Eventually, you will learn what all true leaders learn: vulnerability and personal intimacy are the ultimate tests of your character. For many leaders, this is the last frontier to recognizing what others eventually expect of you—the ability to tell your truth. Unfortunately, for many in leadership roles, this realization comes too late. It's important to remind yourself that every step, every action, and every word you speak will have influence. Your legacy is built on the simple and powerful influence of your ability to be open.

Being open is a powerful form of trust that provides the foundation for mutual respect that resides at the core of all human relationships. Ultimately, keeping one's commitment to being truthful conveys the authenticity, vulnerability, and humility we crave in great leaders. Your legacy will become a permanent portrait of your strengths and good deeds, as well as your failures and flaws. Your legacy will be built one action at a time, giving evidence to how you act in integrity and alignment with the values of trust, honesty, and the sharing of one's truth. For this is the greatest expectation of all.

Chapter Summary

⫻ As a leader, your legacy is defined by the quality of the relationships you have with everyone you touch. It is your life story and conveys the quality of your character and the influence you have on others.

⫻ As a leader, despite perceived unfairness, you will be held to a higher standard.

⫻ The key to trust is keeping your commitments to the people you directly interact with as well as those observing you from afar.

⫻ There are two types of expectations: those that are spoken and those that are unspoken. Unspoken expectations are the slippery slope to disappointment, anger, and resentment.

⫻ Regardless of the relationship, the importance of bringing the unspoken into the spoken realm should never be underestimated.

⫻ There are four key unspoken expectations of leaders that you need to be aware of: talking about what no one wants to talk about; facing the elephants; listening; and always speaking your truth, regardless of how difficult it may be.

⫻ Vulnerability and intimacy are the ultimate tests of your character.

Chapter 3

EMBRACING CONFLICT, SEIZING OPPORTUNITY

Conflict is the reason that leadership exists. Truly successful leaders understand and embrace this idea. They realize that conflict is natural and understand the intensity it brings to every relationship and its constant presence in our lives. How you learn to use conflict will determine whether you succeed or not. In and of itself, conflict is neither positive nor negative. Until someone acts on it, it just is. The challenge is to manage it constructively, realizing it as the power and energy of the human imagination and inventiveness that creates a better world. Great leaders are aware of their unique relationship with conflict and realize that without embracing it, they cannot truly lead or be effective. The most successful leaders embrace conflict and seize it as opportunity.

In general, leaders are curious people. They typically think in terms of possibility. If you are courageous in dealing with conflict and you are curious, you will time and again hit the jackpot of opportunity. This is what viewing every conflict as an opportunity is about. Curiosity allows you to question, explore, and eventually discover the possibilities that exist in every conflict. Truly great leaders learn how to uncover the prospect that every conflict offers and apply it to reach higher levels of performance.

The most successful leaders understand that every conflict presents an opportunity. They embrace conflict as the source of great leadership and appreciate the vital role it plays in their success. They learn that conflict is a reflection of real issues that need to be addressed in order to achieve extraordinary performance.

Society, Conflict, and Competition

From a leader's point of view, conflict is a form of competition that provides the foundation for our global business society. It is a foundation that provides the basis for global competition and underpins our social systems.[1]

For the past several centuries, the human race has been engaged in creating a global business society. In the book *True Alignment*, I encouraged readers to consider the notion that we do not live in a capitalist society; rather, that capitalism is a systemic approach to the business society. It is a social system through which we create and deliver goods and services to satisfy our individual and collective desires and needs. Although this is not a new idea, it does remind us that, at the core, the world we have created—and continue to form—is the result of responding to our wants and needs.

Our needs and desires include not only physical safety, health, success, community, and being loved, but also elements of greed and fear that, at some level, exist in all of us. For when we experience even the slightest level of fear of not getting what we need or want, we become aware of and experience our own internal conflict. This conflict is created by the tension between what we believe is and what should or could be; what we have and what we want.

Throughout history, we have manifested an amazing capability for fulfilling our needs and desires. Beginning with the formation of the most basic social arrangements, we have steadily become more sophisticated in creating systems through which we achieve our individual and shared outcomes. The result is today's global business society. In looking at our world through this lens, we realize that conflict is the foundation for the global social system of business. It always has been. In light of our capacities for creative and critical thinking, we continue to get better and better at it.

Today, the majority of the world is engaged in a form of capitalistic democracy, an accepted system of competition wherein business success and the economic well-being of a nation are the central focus of its existence, a structure that promotes government as a business. This is an important dimension to always be conscious of. It reminds you of your responsibility to act in the greater good of the system in which you participate and to be continuously aware of your influence and contributions.

Is It Always About Winning?

When leaders are asked if they like to compete and win, the answer is virtually always yes. At first glance, a leader's purpose or mission in life may not appear as a conflict. Manifesting a vision, building a successful company, or getting any desired result may not immediately present itself as a conflict. Yet they all are. For most leaders, pursuing their outcomes and achieving their desired goals means winning. Achievement, hitting the numbers, reaching goals, continuous improvement, finishing first, and being the best in the marketplace are all synonymous with winning.

For leaders, this raises an all-important question: Is it always about winning? The answer is yes. It is difficult not to see winning in the equation when overcoming obstacles and great odds, facing and defeating challenges, being better today than yesterday, or simply being the best. The truth is that, in the end, winning depends on how it is defined. For Martin Luther King and President Lyndon Johnson, the definition of winning was attaining equal rights for all the citizens of the United States. For Steve Jobs, winning was to "To make a contribution to the world by making tools for the mind that advance humankind." A couple more examples are the efforts of Whole Foods CEO John Mackey to challenge the readily-accepted views of capitalism that a leader's only responsibility is delivering profit to shareholders. Mackey's win is for leaders to embrace the paradigm of conscious capitalism. At the same time, his aim is to lead his company to succeed in winning the hearts and minds of customers and be the world's largest natural foods grocer.

For the British mathematician and computer scientist Alan Turning, winning meant inventing the techniques and technology to crack German codes to help win a World War. It was also about finding ways to win the approval of people to convince them of the value of artificial intelligence and what it was capable of contributing to humanity. In the early 1960s, in the context of America's conflict with Russia, success was further defined by winning the space race. For the leaders of Wal-Mart, winning is defined by gaining market share through "saving people money so they can live better." For Nelson Mandela, winning was dismantling the legacy of South Africa's apartheid and fostering racial reconciliation. For Mandela, compassion, empathy, and understanding became ways to win.

The definitions of winning appear to be infinite. Certainly, leaders are best served when winning means being in the service of a greater good and cause; when winning represents a deeper human meaning or greater social good. As an aspect of human nature, there will always be a measurement of success that leaders and those that follow them will need. In some form or another, winning is a part of the equation, regardless of how honorable or decent the cause.

For example, the Chief Executive of a healthcare center wants to bring the best pre-eminent care to patients. Doing so and being successful as an organization will be to the benefit of every patient. Furthermore, if the organization serves each and every individual patient well, the entire community will benefit. In order to accomplish its mission, it must meet its goals of attracting enough new patients, thereby also increasing its revenue and profits, and attracting other new resources. To do so, it must also have the support of the physicians in the community that will refer their patients to the organization. As the CEO concluded, "In order to be successful in our mission, we have to generate more revenue. In order to accomplish that, we have to go out and win market share from our competitors." As noble as the mission is, it requires winning.

In one form or another, our definitions of success will reflect a measurement. Call it a scorecard, continuous improvement measurement, a tally of votes, key performance indicators, or simply the bottom line, we want and need proof of success. Why? Because we want to know we're winning. We want to know that the challenge has been met, the malicious forces have been beaten, and that good triumphs evil. We also want to know that our team is winning the game; that we are doing better today than yesterday or, as in the case of the healthcare organization, that we're taking market share from our competitors. This is why, for many leaders, having a nemesis in a marketplace becomes a powerful motivation. It is also a powerful form of motivation for the people in the organizations they lead. Given a choice, most people would pick being a member of a winning team.

The need and passion for competition is driven by the underlying desire to be competent and from a sense of fulfillment that comes from being good at something. It is this innate desire to be competent that naturally emerges through competitive behaviors. Winning provides you with verification that you can be as good as or better than others which, in turn, motivates you to continuously achieve higher results. Keeping track of and scoring your accomplishments—improving on and outdoing your deeds—satisfies your appetite to win.

Leaders display and use their desire to win to influence others to join them in their conflicts. This does not mean that leaders will always want to have it their way. Some of the traits that we look for in great leaders include the ability to collaborate, solve problems with others, and build relationships that reach far beyond the frameworks of winning and losing. I am often asked if a person's desire to win can get in the way of collaboration and partnerships. The answer is yes. We have all experienced a time in our lives when, no matter how much we ask someone to collaborate for mutual benefit, they are not interested. They are only attentive to getting their benefit. No doubt, you must be aware when too much focus on your own needs gets in the way of a win-win outcome that benefits all those involved. When necessary, it is important for you to engage with others to create shared forms and definitions for winning. We look for leaders who engage us in winning together and who understand the importance of mutual benefit. Working toward creating mutual benefit will also enable you to inspire others to find and leverage sources of critical thinking, creativity, and innovation that often go far beyond your own.

The Source of Innovation and Creativity

It's difficult to find a leader that doesn't want to have an organization or team with a culture of innovation, a culture in which its members are demonstrating and freely expressing their creativity. There are multitudes of Websites and books on the topic of innovation. Many of the leading business and management periodicals (*Fast Company, Businessweek, Inc., Harvard Business Review*) devote a great deal of attention to innovation. Several periodicals host conferences on innovation and give awards to the year's most innovative companies, organizations, and leaders. As well, there a host of consultants and leadership coaches offering help for leaders and their organizations to become more innovative.

In my experience, most leaders expect the people they lead to be creative and innovative. Yet I often find that they don't take much time to reflect on what they are asking for. To fully leverage innovation and creativity, it is imperative that you first understand what each is and appreciate how they manifest. After all, for one leader innovation may mean approaching a problem analytically and, by using available data, developing a new process or stem through which to resolve it. For another leader, however, it may mean freewheeling thinking and risk-taking.

The definition for creativity is the ability to make new things or think of new ideas. We often associate creativity to art. As examples, creativity is expressed in painting, music, and film. These are forms of artistic creativity exhibiting the expression of emotion that conveys the underlying need or desire that motivates it. This is why art is so captivating. The more creatively the feeling is expressed, the more we respond and connect to it.

What is just as interesting is that creative emotion is caused by a tension that results when a person's need or desire goes unmet. The craving and want for love and affection, of wanting to be right, or simply wanting respect are all sources of internal conflict that fuel creativity. This also occurs when we engage one another creatively. We use the tensions of conflict to express our ideas and build on them together, leveraging the conflict to higher levels of creativity.

The methods of creativity also apply to innovation. Like creativity, an innovation is best defined as a new idea and as the act of conveying it. Among others, the idea may take the shape of a new device, method, product, process, or insight. All too often, the credit for an innovation is given to a single person. Usually, however, the innovation is the result of a group or team effort, relying on the ability of its members to openly and collaboratively challenge one another and their ideas.

When leaders recognize the source of innovation, they realize the value that constructive conflict brings to the table. For without some type of conflict, the innovation they seek from their organizations and teams would not be possible. Regardless of how uncomfortable you may be with conflict, you will eventually recognize it as the natural result of bright and committed people working with one another. You will see that conflict challenges and offers people the opportunity to learn and grow. It leverages the energy residing in the diversity of thinking and the spectrum of values and beliefs that each individual has to offer. To become a truly successful leader will require you to embrace conflict as an essential ingredient in the innovation and creativity you seek from the people you lead.

There is no shortage of conflict in our world and there never will be. Therefore, there will never be a shortage of opportunity for you to engage others to innovate and bring new ideas into the world in constructive ways. The greatest barrier to doing it resides in you. As a leader, you are a member of the minority of people that everyone else looks to with the expectation of constructively confronting the real issues in their teams, organizations, and communities. In the end, if you are unwilling to confront and leverage conflict, the opportunity will be lost. For this reason, your own personal development often represents your greatest opportunity. You must recognize and confront your own doubts and fears. Only then will you fully realize the endless opportunities that conflict presents.

Chapter Summary

⚊ Truly successful leaders understand and embrace that conflict is natural. It is not positive or negative and must be used in constructive ways.

⚊ Great leaders are curious human beings and see every conflict as an opportunity.

⚊ From the leader's point of view, conflict is a form of competition that provides the foundation for our global business society.

⚊ Leaders are best served when their definitions of winning are in service to a greater good and cause.

⚊ The passion for competition is driven by the underlying desire to be competent.

⚊ It is important for leaders to engage others to create shared forms and definitions of winning.

Chapter 4

SPOTTING ELEPHANTS

In the story "Jumbo," the main character Pop is the owner of The Wonder Circus. The circus's feature attraction and recipient of Pop's unfaltering affection is Jumbo the elephant. Pop is a great entertainer, brilliant circus marvel, and excellent salesman. He is also a poor businessman. More unfortunately, he is a gambler. After a series of losses from playing craps, and burdened with a pile of IOUs, he is eventually served papers by the local sheriff and loses his circus to a scheming creditor, a much more successful competitor whose only interest is gaining ownership of Pop's circus. Similar to the stories of many business acquisitions, Pop ignores his steady and rising debt and it catches up with him. The sad outcome is that Pop and his family lose their business.

In an effort to carry on, the family forms a traveling carnival, only to find that the show isn't the same without the elephant. When Pop attempts to retrieve Jumbo by sneaking him off the circus grounds, he is confronted by the sheriff who asks, "Where are you going with that elephant?" Caught red-handed, a straight-faced Pop casually replies, "Elephant? What elephant?"

Like many leaders, when confronted with difficult issues and conflict, Pop chose to avoid them. As the situation worsened, he simply hoped that sooner or later his luck would change, his problems would solve themselves, or they would just go away. Along with Pop, the people around him also let the situation continually worsen. They too failed to confront the circumstances and, by not challenging Pop, contributed to the fiasco. Even worse, they continuously let him off the hook. Whether through false hope, positive procrastination, or a false sense of reality, Pop and his followers chose to avoid the elephants in his business. Nor did anyone confront Pop's addiction to gambling, his poor business practices, and his self-deceptive behavior, all of which contributed to his bad decisions and eventual decline of his business.

Despite all the signs, everyone went along with Pop's actions, decisions, and dysfunctions, further encouraging his poor leadership. As often happens in business, even the person closest to him, his daughter, failed to confront him. Whether she thought that avoiding the problems would benefit everyone or she was blinded by her affection, she also chose to avoid confronting the problems faced by the family and the business.

Like many leaders, Pop eventually took on the role of the elephant, which encouraged others to also avoid facing conflict. As we all know from experience, sooner or later even the smallest of ignored issues and conflicts grow to become elephants. In other words, when avoided long enough, even a baby elephant in the corner of the room will become a big elephant.

Whether appearing as a problem, a contentious issue, a disagreement, or a hidden dissatisfaction, sooner or later the elephants come to light. First, one or two people engage in the conflict. Then others find out and more people get involved. Yet, despite knowing better, for one reason or another they deliberately ignore it. There is a fear that keeps the conflict from being confronted and openly discussed. The reasons for this include shame from acting unethically, failing to perform, a truth that puts a relationship at risk, or denying abuse or injustice. Even the bystanders who see the elephant can, for a variety of reasons, avoid involvement.

Your elephants will come in many forms. Though they are often obvious, they can be difficult to spot, well hidden, and elusive. Among the ways they can show themselves include avoided differences in values and beliefs, unclear expectations, unmet commitments and promises, withheld information, dishonesty, backstabbing, coalition building, blame games, and name-calling. These are just a handful of examples of the elephants that you will ultimately be held accountable for. There are many more.

The Highest Level of Responsibility

To be truly effective as a leader begins with accepting the responsibility for spotting and confronting elephants. When all is said and done, you are fundamentally responsible for bringing attention to the conflicts that can block performance and, at the same time, offer opportunities for the open and constructive exchange of ideas and thinking that results in higher levels of performance. Not confronting dysfunctional conflict only weakens your influence as a leader. Further, by accommodating this behavior, you enable others to engage in the dysfunctional and destructive actions that accompanies it.

There is a difference between seeing this as your highest responsibility and calling it accountability. Often, leaders rely too much on the idea of accountability. This is the ability one has to account for one's actions. Unfortunately, more often than not, we use it in the past tense, asking if one can account for what one has already done. When we shift our thinking to taking responsibility, we take a more active and forward-looking view to having and accepting the ability to respond. This is being mindful to the present and engaging in the moment of truth. Furthermore, when you embrace your responsibility, you find yourself more actively looking for and spotting opportunities to take action. When you ask others to be more proactive, you are asking them to act from a place of accepting responsibility.

As a leader, you are expected and required to constructively face the many conflicts that will naturally exist in your organization or team. Further, to be effective you not only have to respond to the conflicts and issues at hand, you also have to actively look for, identify, and uncover the hidden and avoided conflicts. Ultimately, this is what you will be judged for.

Accepting responsibility to confront conflict will add to your influence in several ways. I have found that openness, confidence, and courage are three essential traits for leaders when confronting conflict:

Openness. By spotting and confronting elephants, you demonstrate your commitment to one of the more powerful core values that we all share. As a leader, you will be tested on this more than any other value. You are expected to openly and honestly express what you think, see, and feel. Though it is obvious that not everyone will always agree with your truth or perspective, the important aspect to remember is that, as a leader, people will want to hear your truth and will appreciate your commitment to honesty. We all recognize that it takes courage to be honest. Our shared knowledge of the fear associated with being honest is key to our understanding the value it brings to trusting one another. As formidable as the fear is, it stands to reason that the honesty to confront it is that much more powerful.

Our experience is that leaders often shy away from expressing themselves honestly; so much so that we have become suspicious, expecting them to lie. More often than not, criticism of how leaders communicate is not focused on competency; rather, it is centered on the lack of transparency. Sadly, we have become too accepting of leaders who lie, withhold the truth, or win our favor through exaggeration. In a world where we critique every action and every word, the truth is that leaders who commit to honesty are rare and, for that reason, are considered even more extraordinary. This is to your advantage.

Confidence. Leaders that are responsible in confronting conflict gain not only confidence in themselves, but also that of others. We admire individuals who are willing to tell the truth and point out the elephant in the room. Often, when no one else is willing to do it, the first person that is brave and confident enough to confront the situation gains the influence to become the leader. Eventually, we have confidence that the leader will act when we need him or her to.

One of the keys to taking action is knowing when to act. Often, leaders shy away from confrontation because they aren't sure of saying the right things or having the right solution. It is more important to show integrity by telling others that, though you don't have a solution to the problem at hand, you intend to simply bring attention to the issue. Doing so also encourages others to engage in the conversation.

When spotting elephants, it is vital to keep in mind that even if you don't have a solution or you misstep in communicating your truth, you will still be delivering on your responsibility to face the most difficult of situations. By doing so, you will learn how to manage difficult circumstances better and add to your own confidence. If you don't get it right the first time, the big payoff is that you can use the experience to learn and grow. Also, being consistently honest and responsible about an uncertain resulting action or outcome will inspire the confidence of others. Your predictability will make them feel safe in times of great anxiety and fear.

Keep in mind that leadership is an art. Like any art form, it requires taking risks and getting better through practice. Although it may be difficult at first, with time you'll find that committing to spotting elephants and truthfully confronting the conflicts they represent is the key to your success as a leader.

Courage. Great leaders are the role models of courage. By spotting and confronting elephants, they set the expectation that others will do the same. Further, if you do it well, others will learn from observing you and follow your lead. They, too, will then want to show courage.

We often see great leadership as the ability to solve problems. No doubt this is an important characteristic of successful leaders. I suggest that even more important is the ability to spot the opportunities that, when leveraged, provide for the possibility to confront a problem and address it in a manner that leads to higher levels of performance. Such role modeling gives others examples of the variety of outcomes that spotting elephants can present. It provides the means through which they can explore the virtually endless forms of personal, team, and organizational performance that can be attained.

Role modeling courage and a commitment to honesty evoke traits and characteristics of great leadership and inspire others in spotting the elephants. Among these traits are ownership, conscientiousness, continuous learning, curiosity, and the pursuit of self-knowledge. All of these are positive examples of the outcomes of confronting and leveraging conflict. For those who want to become leaders, your role modeling will encourage them to learn and practice being more courageous, creative, and responsible. In the end, they too will become role models.

Lastly, great leadership that role models how to spot elephants is likely the most powerful and important influence on the culture of organizations, teams, and communities. As we will explore in Chapter 5, a leader's commitment to spotting and confronting elephants will encourage and influence those they lead to do the same in their organizations and teams. In doing so, they will contribute to managing the most critical aspect of their work cultures.

Real Issues, Real Emotions

I often like to share with audiences the idea that we live with a fair number of fallacies. On a worldwide basis and across all geographic and religious cultures, the most commonly accepted fallacy is that the sun rises. It doesn't; the Earth turns. The second misconception that we accept is what I like to refer to as the "don't take this personally" fallacy. I find this to be impossible for anyone to truly accomplish. After all, every interaction and every moment of our lives is a personal experience. We filter and gauge every experience through our self-concept, our values and beliefs, our histories, and our view and perceptions of life. They are the ingredients and provide the context through which we live, relive, and tell our stories. Everything is personal.[1]

It is because we take everything personally that makes confronting conflict as uncomfortable and unpredictable as it is. What makes issues real is the emotion that accompanies them because they are personal. In most instances, it is the source of emotion that creates the issue. As a leader, it is a profoundly powerful dimension of human behavior and interaction to be aware of and better understand.

Too often, it is what we perceive as the emotional aspect of our interactions with others that makes us uncomfortable. It is why we are naturally so willing to avoid conflict. If this is true, it also stands to reason that one of the best ways to go elephant spotting is to look for situations in which there is emotion. This is not easy because the emotions and accompanying behaviors such as anger and resentment make us uncomfortable. Often they are the prickly, dysfunctional, combative, and vindictive behaviors we associate with conflict.

As a leader looking to spot elephants, such emotional behaviors are evidence that you are on the right path. Strong emotions are almost always indicators of real issues.

Chapter Summary

✎ Being truly effective as a leader begins with accepting your responsibility for spotting and confronting conflict.

✎ Avoiding dysfunctional conflict not only weakens your influence as a leader, it also enables dysfunction and unproductive behaviors.

✎ There are three traits that great leaders consistently display in confronting conflict: openness, confidence, and courage.

✎ Leaders that confront conflict gain not only confidence in themselves, but also gain the confidence of others.

✎ Like any art form, leadership requires you to take risks. The only way to get better is through practice.

✎ It is because we take everything personally that conflict feels uncomfortable and unpredictable.

✎ As a leader looking to spot elephants, it helps to remember that real emotions are almost always indicators of real issues.

Chapter 5

ELEPHANTS OF MANY COLORS

Regardless of how present the elephant may be, there will almost always be people trying to avoid it and keep it hidden. This is especially true of the parties directly engaged in the conflict. Sometimes the elephant in hiding exists without outward or easy-to-recognize emotional behavior. That makes spotting it very difficult. As the leader, you must be willing to be the tracker who follows the trail and, once you find the elephant in hiding, be willing to confront it, make others aware of it, and discover its root cause. Therein lies the opportunity.

One of the greatest challenges you will face is always being able to immediately spot the elephant. When the elephant is not spotted, or the hidden rule of avoidance takes over, it manifests into a problem that can consume a team and even an entire organization. If left unrecognized and unchallenged, the conflict and the accepted story grow into the dysfunction that lays claim to a culture. Once an elephant takes hold, it becomes the guide that people follow to play politics—the games of power and influence—that threaten an organization and interfere in its performance. It lives in the patterns of behavior that undermine a healthy culture. With time, the elephants become not only difficult to see, but also more difficult to confront and discuss.

Every organization has its own unique culture. And every culture can have its own definitions of dysfunctional actions, a root cause and set of behaviors that explains and permits a departure from what is considered normal, acceptable, or satisfactory. Every culture can fall prey to norms of obsession and compulsive behavior that can have a negative or destructive effect on its members. All organizations or groups have the ability, at some level, to engage in patterns of behavior that solicit fear and anxiety.

On the surface, you will see evidence of the conflicts and how they manifest. It's relatively easy to spot the "us vs. them" coalition forming. In some instances, the coalition building can spur competition that elevates creativity which, if led in the right direction, can be productive. Unfortunately, this creative energy can also be applied to unproductive means of competition, resulting in groups or teams at odds with one another. The patterns that emerge can often result in a lack of collaboration or teamwork, the "over-the-wall" tossing of unresolved problems, finger pointing and blame, and the withholding of information and critical resources. Sadly, several of these forms of coalitions playing off one another can be used as sabotage.

With time, such coalitions can take hold and be passed on to new members of teams and groups resulting in continuing battles. For example, I recently met with an executive who had just joined the company team. After 60 days of joining the company, he already had a good idea of which conflicts were already at play and was becoming versed at knowing the rules. He was already able to tell me who the main characters in the story were, how they were positioned, and which members of the team had support. This is a natural aspect of conflict. When I asked him how he felt about it, he told me he was concerned that he would not be able to accomplish what he was hired for. He also told me that he had to be very careful to "not get caught in the middle."

People naturally find others to support and verify their points of view. From time to time, we all do it. We want to know that we are in the right, know better, or have the better way. It's human nature to find others to help us draw the line and try to win. What starts as a disagreement or distrust between two people can eventually become a deeply embedded dysfunctional feud between two groups. In many cases, it is leaders that build the coalitions. It is no wonder that they can be maintained for long periods of time. The coalitions become sources of power and influence, but not just for leaders. Members of the coalitions gain the influence of connective power and a sense of inclusion. They will get their own needs for significance, control, and acceptance met through enrolling in the conflict, despite how negative and unproductive it may turn out to be. Without being confronted, the coalitions become a platform for a host of other dysfunctional norms and barriers to success.

For the purpose of providing you with recognizable examples, the following is a list of dysfunctions that are common elephants. I invite you to add to the list.[1] Elephants come in many colors. In no particular order or rank, the following are commonly identified elephants:

#1 – *Emotional abuse.* This includes name-calling, bullying, and the use of profanity to intimidate others and keep them on the defensive. The more subtle approach is constant criticism and labeling. Such criticism can be delivered in a direct manner or can be veiled as challenges to new ideas or asking others to always exceed expectations. Or, it takes place through third parties and through the indirect means of hurtful innuendo and gossip.

I have also observed abusive and sadistic behavior disguised as "brutal honesty," a form of alleged constructive feedback or frankness. Using honesty as a way to communicate in a constructive manner is very different from using it as weapon of aggressive force, threat, or putting others down.

#2 – *Victimhood.* This pattern of conduct is aimed at gaining and holding the attention of others and often manifests through people playing the role of the "poor, pitiful" characters who are in constant need of attention and for whom no solution ever works, never completely solves their problem, or satisfies their hunger for attention. Unfortunately, the victims rarely take responsibility or accountability for their own outcomes and performance, and will easily blame someone else or the circumstances of their environment.

Victimhood takes up a great deal of attention and energy from others. Needless to say, if a leader takes on the role of victim, a group, team, and even the entire organization can fall into the trappings of being victims together. This includes accepting failure and always blaming everyone but themselves.

#3 – *Ignoring boundaries.* Going beyond the boundaries is a form of behavior that ignores the values and beliefs of the organization or community. Beyond mere rebellion against the rules, individuals who ignore the values and beliefs of an organization are typically acting in a manner that tests the culture's tolerance and may eventually get ostracized or excluded. Unfortunately, when a leader and culture fails to confront this behavior, coalitions of "us vs. them" are formed and tolerated. Often, such patterns are maintained for long periods of time and the conflicts are handed down from those who started the conflicts to those who newly enter the organization and, knowingly or unknowingly, accept them.

#4 – *Baiting.* One of the more common forms of dysfunction that is tolerated or ignored is intentional baiting to get an emotional response. Often, under the guise of challenging others, individuals will knowingly induce an argument or disagreement just to engage in a squabble. Although this can be seen as merely a desire to be combative and argumentative, it is also usually used to deflect or redirect from a real conflict or issue. Often, I have observed this as a form of intentional conflict to keep another motive or action hidden. In some cases, someone baiting and keeping you in an argumentative state does so to hold your attention, thus reinforcing his or her sense of importance.

#5 – *Old conflicts.* In some instances, individuals derive importance and influence by keeping old conflicts alive. In such cases, they become historians holding on to past characters and ideas, thus resisting change. The lack of willingness to move forward or accept resolutions to old conflicts can show up in a variety of ways. Whatever the underlying motivation, old battles will continue to draw and enlist new advocates and fighters. The real problem is the exorbitant amount of time and energy wasted in the present on keeping an old conflict alive.

Whether it is from a past issue of unmet mutual benefit, resisting change, or an unacceptable resolution to a previous conflict, ongoing anger and resentment for unresolved issues will eventually manifest in an assortment of negative and destructive behaviors. These can include sabotage, backstabbing, and apathy. Overcoming these negative behaviors gives you good reason to confront old conflicts, regardless of how insignificant they may appear.

Such conflicts become a part of the hidden or unspoken rules. They are shared through underground signals and covert communication until they are brought to light through a sudden release of pent-up anger. Unfortunately, to be an accepted member of an organization often requires the keeping of family secrets.

#6 – *Withholding information.* Not sharing information and knowledge is likely the most common form of passive-aggressive behavior. Because withholding information is readily defined as lying by omission, it typically results in higher levels of distrust. People will withhold information for a variety of reasons, none of which are usually good. The long-standing view is that information and knowledge are power, which are also necessities for identifying and solving problems. Among others, the motivations to withholding information include retaliation, obsessive competition, sabotage through letting others fail, selfishness, the risk of rejection, and drawing attention for self-value and aggrandizement. Too often we see that withholding of information and knowledge prevents teams and organizations from attaining the levels of trust and commitment necessary to perform well.

#7 – *Abuse of rank*. One of the more common forms of dysfunction is the excessive use of power that accompanies a rank or position in the hierarchy and which can drive levels of fear, distrust, and lack of motivation. Typically, the underlying motivation is the need for control. Along with micromanagement, abuse of rank also manifests as favoritism, "good ol' boy" networks, tightly controlled circles of influence, and the misuse of reward systems.

When rank is used as a source of fear and manipulation, it will eventually result in people doing only what is necessary to get along and feel safe. Doing anything else is taking unnecessary risk. It will certainly prevent feedback and information from reaching those in charge.

#8 – *Gossip*. Whether this manifests as over-sharing of information or self-importance from being at the social center, gossiping creates drama. In either case, it brings little value to an organization or team and has potentially devastating effects. This includes false accusations and damaging people's reputations, undermining an organization's strategies, and broadcasting inaccurate information that can create anxiety and fear. In the end, gossip, rumors, lies, half-truths, and speculation will only serve those who crave significance, attention, or belonging to the in-group.

#9 – *You owe me*. Although mutual benefit and reciprocity are key ingredients to trusting relationships, doing things for one another with strings attached can quickly erode them. As a typical form of negative manipulation, when leaders and people in organizations operate under the premise that everything has a price, resentment is sure to be present. Such resentment manifests as fear and anger and emanates from an imbalanced power in relationships that leaves many with a perceived lack of control. Like selling one's soul to the devil, those who are indebted may be asked to do something that is not aligned to their values and beliefs.

#10 – *Over-harmonizing.* It would be a disservice on my part to ignore over-harmonizing, as this is another common dysfunction. A close kin to "no-tell" and "no-talk" rules that exist in almost any organization or team, over-harmonizing is one dysfunction that can be the cover up to the first nine in this list. A form of protecting each other, this is typically framed as acting in the "greater good" and to the benefit of one another. The fact is that over-harmonizing allows people to ignore and avoid conflict. Poor performance, a lack of responsibility, unethical acts, unmet results, poor financial results, taboos, and a lack of leadership can all fall under the umbrella of false proclamations that everything is all right and nothing needs to be discussed. Through positive procrastination, people grant permission to one another to go blindly forward, all ignoring the elephant. They wait, hoping it will simply leave. In the meantime, they ignore and feed it as it grows.

A CEO once asked me why some organizations can't seem to deal with passive-aggressive behavior. In my experience, I have found that the cause almost always traces back to the leader. If the leader is avoiding the conflicts of the organization or team, he or she is directly engaging in a form of passive-aggressive behavior. Though it could be unintentional, if the leader is aware of a conflict and avoids facing it, he or she will encourage others to act in passive-aggressive ways.

Some dysfunctions are readily identifiable and others are more hidden. When a leader fails to confront one, it may re-surface in different forms. Much like symptoms of a disease that goes untreated, it will inevitably appear through other symptoms, acting like a cancer that grows and eventually wreaks havoc throughout a company. The waste of time and resources, the lack of productivity, and the lost opportunities that are missed due to avoided conflict cost our businesses billions of dollars and results in disappointment in our organizations and distrust of those leading them. It pays to pay attention.

An elephant living in a zoo consumes 250 to 350 pounds of food and more than 45 gallons of water per day. In the wild, one elephant can eat as much as 600 pounds per day. That's a lot of energy being consumed and it's only one elephant. Not to mention what it leaves behind: on average, one elephant will produce over 85,000 pounds of manure per year. That's quite a big mess.

There's another powerful aspect of spotting elephants. If you don't learn to spot elephants, you will not discover your own contribution to creating them. One of the great discomforts leaders face in confronting the elephant is when they themselves are a part of it. Like any human being, you will be motivated by the need to fit in with the norms of the culture of your organization or team. Like anyone else looking to fit in, conflicts offer leaders ways to take part in and gain acceptance of the groups and teams they lead. After all, conflicts offer sources of power and influence and part of your role is to learn to exercise that influence. As a result, you can easily participate in a dysfunction that is considered normal and accepted behavior.

It's too easy to take part in sustaining a conflict that already exists. If you are not actively looking to spot the elephants and are unaware of their existence, you send the signals through your passive behavior that permits others to continue feeding the elephant. You may even find yourself contributing to and participating in giving birth to a new elephant. The reality is that if you're not paying attention, it becomes a trap that you can easily fall into. When you do, in light of your role and influence, and whether you like it or not, you assume responsibility for it. As a leader, the last thing you want to do is take on the role of the elephant.

Chapter Summary

⚖ Regardless of how present the elephant is, there will almost always be people avoiding it and keeping it hidden.

⚖ It's not easy to spot the elephant in the boardroom when it is you.

⚖ If avoidance takes over, it manifests into an elephant that can embed itself in your culture, encouraging others to take part in company politics.

⚖ Every culture can fall prey to obsessive and compulsive behavior.

⚖ It is human nature to find others to help and support us in our conflicts.

⚖ Among the dysfunctions of conflict are: emotional abuse; victimhood; ignoring boundaries; baiting; old conflicts; withholding information; abuse of rank; gossip; "you owe me" thinking; and over-harmonizing.

⚖ The waste of time and resources, the lack of productivity, and the lost opportunities that are missed due to avoided conflict cost our businesses and economies billions of dollars.

⚖ If you don't learn to spot elephants, you will not discover your contribution to creating them.

Chapter 6

CULTURES OF INNOVATION

Among leaders, the attention being paid to the significance of culture is at an all-time high. It is evidence that culture has taken its rightful place as a key priority of great leadership. The notions that culture trumps everything else, eats strategy for breakfast, and is the main ingredient in the success or failure of a business are all confirmation of the now-accepted reality that a healthy culture is necessary for innovation and higher levels of performance. That makes the intentional leadership of culture a must-have skill for you as a leader.

Defining what an innovative culture is creates a challenge for you to go beyond the accepted models of organizations that have been prevalent in the past and still are today. These accepted models include cultures that pressure people to keep playing the game, adhering to rigid rules, protecting the inner circle of power, and keeping real issues and conflicts at bay.

Linking Conflict to Innovation

Recognizing and understanding the link of conflict to innovation is a key to leading your culture to achieve higher levels of success. For this purpose, it is imperative to become an astute student of culture. As a leader, you will find that intentionally leading a culture is hard work and will present you with some of your most demanding challenges. Although there are many, I will discuss four challenges that can frequently get in the way of creating and developing an innovative culture.

The first challenge is that most of what you learn about culture comes through trial and error. Like most leaders, until you find yourself in a predicament of necessity, you will likely not devote much time and energy to learning about culture or developing your expertise. You probably only focus on culture when you have to, when the conflicts become too painful to ignore, and learning as you go.

The second challenge is that you may struggle with leading culture because you don't have a measurable and observable framework for defining it. The traits and characteristics of culture go far beyond the articulation and communication of your organization's core values. In the book *True Alignment*, I list a set of 12 traits and characteristics that provide insight into how people interact and work with one another to get things done, including what is considered acceptable and unacceptable behavior: Power and Influence; Planning and Goal Setting; Problem Solving; Decision Making; Conflict Management; Incentive and Reward; Hiring; Role Definition; Customer Interface; Teamwork; Structure; and Aligned Values. A closer look at the list reveals that they all, in one way or another, address the natural conflicts that arise.[1]

The third challenge is that leaders don't typically see conflict as the most telling way to interpret how their culture actually works. Take a step back and you'll quickly discover that the reason we engage in developing organizations and team building is to more effectively manage conflict. Every culture has a price of admission. No doubt, talent and competency, the ability to be a team player, and authenticity are important to being successful in any culture. That being said, the true price of admission to any culture is in knowing how to align your behavior to what is expected of you, especially in a conflict situation.

For example, Mary is the new Vice President of Marketing. During a meeting of the executive team, she shares an idea that the CEO responds to negatively. The CEO explains that the proposed strategy is one that the company has tried to implement before and has not had success with. Mary tells the CEO that "with due respect" this time "he may be wrong." She assertively argues that her approach is cutting-edge, worked at the last company she implemented it in, and that with the CEO's and team's support, the strategy will succeed. When the CEO gives her a skeptical look, she explains that he and the rest of the leadership team likely have not come across it before. She believes her role is to push the envelope and bring new ways of thinking to the company. After all, this is why she was hired. The rest of the team does not share any further opinions and the CEO explains to Mary that, in the end, he will have final say on such matters. He tells Mary to go back to the drawing board to find another, better strategy that the team will agree with.

Following the meeting, Dan, the head of R&D, catches up to Mary in the hallway and asks her if she is all right. Mary confides in him that she is disappointed. She explains that she didn't feel the CEO was interested in her point of view or willing to listen to her. She is disappointed no one else on the team spoke up. Dan explains that the way she approached her disagreement with the CEO is not "the way we do things around here." He tells her, "We don't confront one another like that in our meetings. Those kinds of conversations are held behind closed doors. Especially when it comes to the CEO." He suggests to her that, in the future, if she wants a better chance of convincing him of her point of view, she would be best served to get her talking points all lined up and ask for a private one-on-one meeting with the CEO.

When it comes to conflict and the rules of engagement, knowing how to present one's point of view will often have as much to do with one's success as having a good rationalization or argument. In this first example, how conflict is managed is the way in which the team experiences innovation. That doesn't necessarily make it bad. What matters most is whether the team and the organization can achieve the levels of creativity, change, and performance that it desires.

Here is another way the same type of scenario could play out differently. Mary, the new VP of marketing is participating in a meeting of the leadership team. During the meeting, the CEO announces that he has some new ideas for the branding effort of the company. He shares them with the group, adding that he just finished reading a book on how several other companies succeeded in establishing their own brands in the same way. From her experience, Mary thinks that his ideas are off track and very difficult to accomplish in their specific marketplace. Rather than speaking up in the meeting, she hopes to find the right opening to privately speak with the CEO.

Following the team meeting, Mary shares her thoughts and ideas with Dan, the head of R&D. She also asks him if he would be willing to help her make her case to the CEO. Dan explains to Mary that when any member of the team has a disagreement with another member, including the CEO, they "talk about it right then and there in the meeting. We don't hold our punches and are open to each other's opinions. The worst thing you can do is to not speak up or have a conversation without having everyone involved. We confront all of our disagreements in the group. It's the way we do things around here. If you're going to be successful, I suggest you learn how to do it." In this example, the path to innovation is for members of the team to confront each other and openly disclose their disagreements and differing views during their meetings. As he does in the first example, Dan is teaching Mary about the price of admission and how they engage in the creativity that results in the innovation and performance the team desires. It looks very different.

The fourth challenge is that most leaders will let others learn what is expected of them through trial and error. This is a common issue that can be easily rectified by leaders clearly articulating how they want members of their organizations to manage conflict. It is difficult to have a culture of innovation without people knowing what it looks like.

Conflict is the natural fuel for innovation. Using it effectively is the responsibility of the leader. It is worth repeating that every conflict is an opportunity that requires you, as leader, to leverage for critical thinking, creativity, and innovation. Here are some reminders of how you can be more effective in leading your work culture:

- Embrace conflict as the source of innovation that manifests the patterns and norms of a healthy culture.

- Become an avid and astute student of culture. Learn everything you can about it and focus on building your competencies and skills, and especially on how to constructively use conflict.

- Don't rely on trial and error. Culture and innovation are much too important to leave to chance. Set expectations and learn to assess which behaviors are aligned with the various aspects of your culture, including conflict management, problem solving, decision making, and sharing feedback with one another.

- As a leader, it is your responsibility to articulate, teach, and coach the members of your culture in the effective management and use of conflict. Everyone needs to have a clear understanding of what is being asked of them, enabling them to act in alignment with your culture's unique definition of innovation.

Cultures Follow Leaders

There is an intimate and undeniable bond between leadership and culture. To this relationship we add conflict. As the old saying goes, as the leader does, so does the culture. As much as your vision, values and beliefs, and drive for success will influence the culture of your organization or team, it stands to reason that your personality traits, strengths, and preferences will also have an influence on your culture. Your strengths and positive characteristics will influence how people behave. Your problems also eventually become the problems and dysfunctions of the culture. Saying that you are responsible for culture is a huge understatement. As a leader, if you do not intentionally shape the culture, someone else will.

When it comes to leading and shaping culture, there are three aspects that you will need to be aware of and use wisely: role modeling, reinforcement, and the influence of your reputation.

Role modeling. As a leader, the cultural influence you derive from role modeling should not be overlooked. We often see leaders who do not act in alignment with the values and beliefs they espouse. Regardless of whether you like the attention or not, because you are the leader, people will always be watching and paying attention to the things you do and say. Every action you take will send some kind of a message. This goes beyond the notion that your actions will speak louder than your words. Your words are also actions. Looking to you for the signals of what to do and not, those you lead will be influenced by even the smallest of nuances of what you say and how you say it.

There is a deep psychological link between your leadership and how your culture manages and uses conflict. Your approach is most often the one that people surrounding you will take. Whether they like it or not is typically less important than the sense of safety that comes from the predictability of knowing how to behave. As human beings, we want to feel safe and know that we do not have to deal with the emotional burden of fear. If you are the type of leader that avoids conflict, you are giving everyone around you the permission to evade it. If you are blaming, you are granting the people in your culture permission to be accusing. If you are open and accept responsibility, you are inviting others to be open and accepting of their responsibilities.

If you are over-demanding and always insisting on having it your way, you'll likely find that others in leadership positions doing the same thing. Over-controlling leadership behavior can quickly permeate a culture to the point where it is not only suppressive, but so rigid that it interferes with critical thinking and leaves people compliant instead of committed to reaching higher levels of performance. This is a far cry from how people function and perform when they act out of a sense of flexibility, openness, and freedom from tight control over their roles and actions.

If you are curious and ask questions to understand others, you are letting them see that you welcome and value their curiosity. If you are closed and never explore, you will be giving others the permission to behave the same. If you act embarrassed and defensive when you lack competency, then others will shy away from acknowledging their own incompetence and will not ask for help when they need it. On the other hand, when you willingly acknowledge your incompetency, you create an environment where others feel safe to ask for help.

If you act selfishly and only look out for your own benefits and gains, others will follow your lead and avoid the opportunities to create mutual benefit. If you act to ensure the mutual benefits of those around you, others will do the same, guaranteeing that everyone benefits, including you.

Reinforcing. As a leader, you also have the responsibility to reinforce the behaviors that are acceptable and unacceptable. You reinforce behavior in two ways: actively and passively. Active reinforcement is where you acknowledge and talk about the behavior, making it clear which behaviors and actions align with the culture, including its values, beliefs, and how things get done. Unfortunately, many leaders will fail to leverage the aspect of positive reinforcement. This is particularly true when it comes to conflict situations. Because there is no problem or crisis that is evident, it is easy to overlook the actions and influence of people when they are managing and using conflict effectively. When someone is acting in alignment, it is in your best interest to acknowledge it. Letting people know that they are behaving in alignment motivates them to continue acting in the manner that you want them to. Recognizing people publically for their success will reinforce your expectations in managing and using conflict in constructive ways.

Through active reinforcement you also confront situations in which people are not acting in alignment with the values and beliefs of the culture and how they are expected to manage and use conflict. To do this effectively, you must not only acknowledge when people are behaving out of alignment, but also point out the corrections and needed changes in behavior and their responsibility to doing so. As with any conflict situation, you are expected to have the emotional strength and wherewithal to confront the misaligned behavior. If you don't, you not only miss the opportunity to reinforce the need for correction and change in behavior, you also become part of the problem. You are giving permission to those observing the situation to act in the same unacceptable manner that you are.

The other form of reinforcement is of the passive nature. At one time, you were a teenager; we all were. Hence, we all know a little about passive reinforcement in testing and stretching the boundaries. When it comes to passive reinforcement, it is important to understand that when you engage in it, you are silently giving others permission to continue doing what they are doing. Regardless of the positive or negative consequences, your actions tell them it is acceptable.

The problem with passive reinforcement is simply that, as a leader, you are doing it most of the time. Unless you make the conscious choice to engage in active reinforcement, your passive behavior will signal what is acceptable and unacceptable behavior. This means that you'll miss the opportunities to recognize and actively reinforce positive conflict behavior. You will also miss the occasions to actively engage and confront the negative behaviors.

Reputation. As all leaders eventually learn, your reputation depends on how you use and manage conflict. If your reputation is to always win, others will inevitably believe they too can win. If you are rigid, don't be surprised if those who work with you are also rigid and inconsiderate of others' ideas. If you are collaborative and work toward mutually benefitting solutions and outcomes, others will do so as well. By being a good listener, others will acknowledge the importance of listening and become attentive to one another.

Your reputation is what others believe about you, how they feel about you, and what they hold to be true about you. It is the expression of their experience of your personal traits and characteristics. It conveys their trust in you and reflects their perception of your character, esteem, values, and the respect you show others. As a leader, your reputation reflects the sum of the opinions that others have of you as a human being.

The lessons of reputation can often be hard learned. Like trust, it will take time to build your reputation. Like trust, it can be damaged in an instant. In a moment, people will shift their opinion of you and they will influence others to change with them. It will not take you long to draw the thread that connects your reputation to conflict. Your character, values and beliefs, the respect you show for others, your compassion and empathy, and your reasoning to assess situations and seek the truth—all of these elements will be tested. Although the patterns of your behavior will form the foundation of your reputation, there can also be a single moment or event that defines how others see you. Eventually, your reputation informs and becomes a part of your legacy.

Your approach to using and managing conflict is likely the single most powerful influence on the culture you lead. Through your role modeling, reinforcement, and reputation, you define and inform how others should engage one another. This means that you can intentionally work toward creating the patterns of behavior that contribute to establishing a culture that uses conflict to fuel the innovation that you and your organization inevitably need to succeed.

A culture that appreciates elephants not for the obstacles and negativity they represent, but rather as the opportunity to confront conflict in constructive ways will drive the innovation that results in higher levels of success.

Chapter Summary

- Among leaders, the attention being given to the significance of culture is at an all-time high.

- Understanding the link between conflict and innovation is a key to managing your culture to succeed.

- Due to conformity and the lack of open dissention, leaders squelch the creativity and innovation they ask for.

- Producing a culture of innovation creates a challenge for leaders to go beyond the accepted models and ways of doing business that have been prevalent in the past and are often still present today.

- Every culture will have its unique traits and characteristics. None is more telling or more powerful than how it uses and manages conflict.

- Leaders do not typically see conflict as the most telling way of interpreting their culture.

- Constructive use of conflict by the leader and members of the organization makes the culture innovative.

- There is an intimate and undeniable bond between leadership, culture, and conflict. As the saying goes, as the leader does, so does the culture.

- As a leader, if you do not intentionally shape the culture, someone else will.

- Your reputation as a leader is dependent on how you use and manage conflict.

- The lessons of reputation can often be hard learned. Like trust, it will take time to build your reputation. Like trust, it can be damaged in an instant.

- A high performing culture embraces its elephants as opportunities to confront conflict in constructive ways and drive the innovation that results in success.

Chapter 7

LOVING ELEPHANTS

Imagine for a moment that you are the leader of a team of managers. You walk into the meeting room and ask the members of your team to help you identify all the conflicts that need to be talked about and are currently not being confronted.

What do you think would happen? Would they look down? Would they look at one another, waiting for someone to answer your question? Would they make eye contact with you? If they did, what do you imagine you would see in their eyes? Would they tell you that there are no unspoken conflicts? Or, would they begin talking about issues that really matter?

If you've never tried this approach, I would suggest that you do. If no one speaks up, you may not have any issues that need to be addressed. Or, you spotted the first really big elephant: no one is willing to face the truth.

Every Culture Has Its Way

You are unlike anyone else. There is only one you. The traits and characteristics of your personality make you different and unlike anyone else. Yes, there are things you have in common with others. That's the natural consequence of the fact that we are all human beings and have certain traits and characteristics that we all share. And then there are the qualities and peculiarities that set you apart from everyone else and make you unique.

The same holds true for cultures. As I described in the previous chapter, there are characteristics of culture through which we can see what all organizations and teams have in common. They provide us with observable elements through which we can define and describe the patterns and norms of how people participate in them. They also give us a lens through which we can see the uniqueness of each culture and the distinctive ways in which individual organizations and teams function.

Just as you have preferences, behavioral traits, and idiosyncrasies in using and managing conflict, so do cultures. And though there are the more evident patterns of conflict management—such as trying to win, pleasing and accommodating others, acting aggressively or using threat, negotiating to get an advantage, looking for the quick fix or compromise, giving in and being submissive, or inviting others to collaborate and problem solve—there are also traits of behavior and communication that provide the underpinnings for the more obvious approaches. It is through these traits that we can better understand why some cultures fear elephants and others learn to love them.

Cultures that love elephants—those that relentlessly strive to find them—display a number of common characteristics. They include innovation, a vision and focus on results, clearly defined values and beliefs, open communication, and continual assessment on achieving results. Therefore, they consistently achieve higher levels of sustainable performance and results. In the end, the success of these characteristics is reliant on whether the culture has a constructive approach to using and managing conflict effectively.

For example, a leader that I have the good fortune of working with is very clear that she always loves a good challenge. She thrives on them. When we first met and I asked her to tell me about herself, one of the first things she mentioned was her penchant for taking on the most difficult tests. She has kept her word. The more difficult the challenge, the more she engages intellectually and the greater her emotional motivation becomes.

To become more successful, she has worked hard at developing her leadership skills and striving toward always engaging others respectfully and positively. And she continues to learn and grow. She also has the same expectation of others. She is inquisitive, curious, and creative, and expects others to be so. As a result, she naturally created an environment in which people were expected to openly challenge one another's ideas and ways of doing things.

She also quickly learned that applying the same standards to managing and using conflict would benefit the company. As a result, she clearly communicated that the respectful way in which people are expected to take on challenges is the way in which conflicts should be managed. She stressed that everyone in the company should strive toward confronting conflict in a respectful and productive manner, including when others have a conflict with her. This not only made her conscious of potential conflicts, it also allowed her to role model and reinforce how every member of the organization is expected to act. As you might imagine, this had a significant effect on every relationship, including those with the company's customers and vendors.

When I ask people throughout the organization how they describe the values and beliefs of the company, they talk about the level of integrity and respect that everyone conveys to one another and how challenging one other and being curious leads to the innovation the company is known for. When I ask how they accomplish it, they tell me that they rely on their ability to openly challenge one another.

As I inquire how conflict is managed, they explain that challenging someone is not about criticism and blame, but rather about a shared understanding in how to confront the important issues. They see it as a means to test their ideas, assumptions, and differing points of view. When I ask what makes them and others successful, this is often the first thing they tell me about.

As another example, a leader of a company once explained to me that the key to the organization's success relied on the ability of everyone to come together to solve problems. This was particularly true during difficult times, when rallying together became the hallmark of the company's resilience and its aptitude to respond to rapidly shifting market conditions to win more customers. He soon discovered that the same power of teamwork applied to conflict management. With time he found that, though people were expected to talk to one another individually about their differences, bringing together the entire team to uncover their differences and conflicts became the fastest and most effective way to manage and use conflict.

When I asked people in the organization to describe the culture, they talked about collaboration and how everyone strives to get along. They told me that getting along was not achieved by playing it safe and avoiding conflict, but rather by facing issues openly and respectfully, thus strengthening their ability to work together as a team. This is an expectation that everyone has of one another in the company, regardless of their position, level, or the team he or she is a member of.

As the previous examples show, every culture is unique. On the surface, they display similar characteristics. Like their cultures, both leaders are unique. Yet, they also share common leadership traits. At the team and organizational level, both have clearly defined values and beliefs. Members of both of the teams and their companies talk about trust, openness, and the ability to work together well. Openness, confronting conflict, and the capability to collaborate are all spoken expectations that are consistent with the values and beliefs of both cultures.

There is another aspect to their cultures that is often overlooked: both have clearly articulated and demonstrated approaches to teamwork. Though many leaders may talk about teamwork, their organizations will not have clearly defined definitions of this concept. If you look closely at the two companies discussed, whereas they both have the capabilities to confront conflict and collaborate well, there are distinct differences in how the teams go about it. Led by example and well defined expectations from the leader, everyone knows how the team manages and uses conflict to drive individual and collective performance and success.[1]

Speed and Effectiveness

In the previous examples, both cultures and their members exhibit another key characteristic of high performance—speed. They are agile and make changes quickly. This is key for any organization to be innovative and successfully compete in today's fast-changing world. Many leaders talk about having agile, nimble, and proactive cultures and employees. What most do not recognize is that managing conflict is the main driver that makes it all happen.

Two essential characteristics of any high performing culture is the ability to solve problems and make good decisions. This holds true at the organizational, team, and individual level. Although many leaders focus on developing the right processes for making decisions, they soon realize that productive and vigorous decision making is built on openness. It is important to keep in mind that innovation isn't usually the result of a single leap forward. Though it may appear that way to outsiders, innovation is typically accomplished through incremental moments of critical and creative thinking that are fueled by conflict and decisions made a step at a time. It requires a commitment to strong collaboration and openness on the part of everyone involved.

Often, poor decisions are made because information has not been shared with everyone, vital information is missing, or people are misinformed. Whether your definition of collaboration and participation is top-down, bottom-up, or another unique form of decision making, openness is necessary for successful outcomes. When it comes to your culture, openness is also an essential ingredient to speed. When conflict is faced in a timely manner and used as the lever to create change, your team and organization will respond to and engage in creating change faster. This is the kind of speed you seek as a leader. When it comes to bringing the next idea to fruition, as much as any race or conflict you engage in, you will need speed to succeed.

The Competitive Advantage of Listening

There is no one recipe for culture. There is no "one-size-fits-all" approach to doing it right. There are traits that all cultures have in common and markers that separate the high performers from the rest. Among these are the alignment to purpose and vision, a shared vision and aligned strategy, focus on results, teamwork, agility, ingenuity, processes and paths for decision making, and aligned values and beliefs. Without a doubt, these are all important aspects of culture that you need to pay attention to. Each one matters. Yet none matter as much as your ability to engage people with openness and honesty. For without the ability of a company's members to be honest—to express what they think, see, and feel—they will not feel safe to openly engage in the level of creativity that you need from them.

In the two previous examples, the leaders reflect a set of characteristics that are evident and common to both cultures. They include leadership beliefs and behaviors that reinforce the norms of the culture, allowing those they lead to engage in practices that align with the expectation that conflict must be faced. More than any other factor, it is a primary aspect of every person's performance and is the key determinant in whether they are a proper fit for the culture. The expectation is that constructive management of conflict is everyone's responsibility. In both cultures, the leaders also embody openness. This begins with the listening that is the key to the mutual respect, which results in trust and openness.

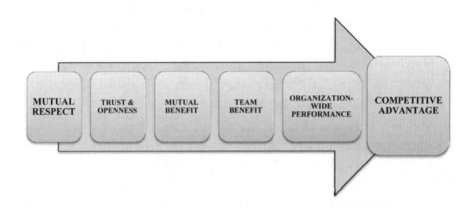

As the previous model demonstrates, the path to great performance begins with establishing mutual respect. Mutual respect means that I treat you in the manner that you want to be treated. In return, you will treat me the way I want to be treated. This is the foundation for trust. Only if I listen to you to understand how you expect me to treat you will you trust my intentions toward you. The same holds true for you listening to me. Listening is the key for openness and honesty in the relationship.

If we have the ability to be open with one another, then we can honestly tell one another if our expectations are not being met. It is natural to engage in conflict if either one of us is not getting our needs met. When this happens and it is ignored, disappointment, resentment, and anger are likely to follow. This makes being open critical to the success of any trusting relationship and creates an ongoing mutual benefit.

It is also what lies at the center of a great team performance. In business we use accountability to describe mutual benefit. Every team member is expected to be accountable for their individual performance in contribution to the success of the entire group. This is the ongoing process of accountability. Only if we listen to one another and work with mutual respect can we constructively confront one another when someone fails to meet a performance expectation or commitment. Needless to say, without mutual respect—without trusting that we will be listened to by one another—this becomes difficult to achieve. In other words, for a team to achieve high levels of performance, its members must be heard by one another, especially when individual goals are not being met and the team's performance is at stake.

Multiply this across the number of teams or groups in an organization and one quickly realizes that the entire enterprise cannot perform to its highest levels without the ability of its members to listen to one another in mutual respect. As a whole, the organization performs well when its members can openly express concerns and issues, knowing and trusting that they will be heard and responded to. When you multiply this effect throughout an organization, you come to realize that mutual respect is a major factor in contributing to its competitive advantage. It is the key to its ability to address conflicts and issues and to innovatively leverage its challenges as opportunities to deliver on its promises, and ultimately, deliver its intention to the customer and win in the marketplace.

Your commitment to listening demonstrates your love of elephants and encourages others to join you in spotting them. This is vital to the performance of your organization. Ultimately, the ability to leverage conflict and listening is an organization's competitive advantage.

To succeed, you need everyone to spot and confront the elephants. This includes having others challenging your competency and admitting when they are more competent and stronger than you. When this happens, you'll find that the most important strength will be their ability to be open, honest, and express their truth. For only then will you be leading a team or organization with a culture that loves to spot the elephants; a culture that is innovative and grabs onto the opportunities of conflict to succeed.

The fear of failure is not about being afraid to fail; it is about your fear to learn about yourself.

Chapter Summary

⫽ Although each organization is unique, there are characteristics of culture that all of them have in common.

⫽ Cultures that love elephants and continuously strive to spot them consistently achieve higher levels of sustainable performance and results.

⫽ Clearly defining how to confront and manage conflict serves everyone on the team and across the organization.

⫽ Innovation is typically accomplished through incremental moments of critical and creative thinking that is fueled by conflict and decisions that are made a step at a time.

⫽ Your entire enterprise cannot perform to its highest levels without the ability of its members to listen to one another in mutual respect.

⫽ Your commitment to listening demonstrates your love of elephants and encourages others to join you in spotting them.

⫽ When it comes to leading a culture of innovation, there's nothing more powerful than openness.

⫽ You will want others to challenge your competency.

⫽ The fear of failure is not about being afraid to fail, but rather about your fear to learn about yourself.

Part II

LEADING THROUGH AWARENESS

Chapter 8

EXPLORING YOUR STORY

As a global society, we have moved through periods of time marked by advances through which we have creatively responded to our needs. Put a challenge in front of us and our capacity to take it on and find a new way to get what we want emerges in powerful forms of innovation. This is human nature at work. Whether it's taking on the threats to our existence, fighting for what we believe is moral and just, or closing a gap between what is and what we think and feel should be, we love a good conflict. We love worthy competition. It makes us want to innovate and bring new ideas and technologies into the world. It makes us hungry for knowledge and drives us to develop ways to get better, striving to improve upon what we've already accomplished.

The various forms of conflict have motivated and elevated us from one period on the historical timeline to the next. It moved us to expand territorially and inspired us to engage in conflicts manifesting in battles and wars over land and resources, differing beliefs, and the desire for economic gain that resulted in the exploration of different parts of the world.

We've continuously created an existence in which our capacity to engage in conflict and competition has resulted in extraordinary technologies that allow us to compete and win at stunning levels. Along with conflict on the battlefield, we now compete economically, outdoing one another in the quest for wealth and emotional fulfillment. The big question is, what is next?

For many, with the advent of social media, the expansive availability of information and knowledge, and the speed through which it is available to access, we are shifting to a time when we must become increasingly aware of how to make good use of it all. As the Information Age evolved into the Digital Age, the innovative technology of the latter has moved us away from face-to-face and personal means of communication, interaction, and dialogue.

With this shift we experienced a number of consequences, good and bad. We now instantly send messages and information to one another around the globe in seconds. We are constantly connected to everyone and everything. We have incredible amounts of information at our fingertips that we can shape, manipulate, and use for ingenious and innovative means.

At the same time, we find ourselves under the duress of being constantly "connected" and stressed in the moments we are not. We find that any message sent to someone can quickly become public knowledge. We are more open to accolades and can achieve instant fame. We are also exposed to criticism and run the risk of immediate and widely broadcast humiliation and shame.

There are also consequences to using technology to publicly air differences, ranging from name-calling and blaming to, in some extreme cases, destroying lives. In organizations, using technology as a substitute for person-to-person, human interaction has reached a critical stage. When this happens, people use technology not only to communicate with one another, but also as a way to avoid confronting issues. Rather than dialogue, some take the easier and less threatening route of engaging in conflicts through e-mail, text messages, and even publically online.

However, we have also come to the point when we can better understand how to use technology constructively to reconnect with our humanity. Many experts view this transition as a time when we must explore, at deeper levels, how what we have created can increase our capacity to understand ourselves.

Called the Age of Awareness, it is a time in history that requires a deeper consciousness of who we are as individuals and what we contribute to a rapidly changing and highly competitive world. Beginning with the responsibility we have to one another, it is a time to individually and collectively discover and explore higher levels of thinking and more mindful human engagement.

This is not an easy undertaking. Relative to the time span of the human race, the broad acceptance of consciousness and cognitive psychology is still new. In light of the complexity and demands for quickly accessing, collecting, and comprehending all the information and knowledge in the world, one cannot discount the necessity to be more aware of our thoughts, motivations, and actions. This is particularly true of leaders.

The ability of leaders to be self-aware has become the most critical aspect of how we judge leaders. It's not hard to identify those who are engaged and motivated by the increased demands of leadership. They are the business and social leaders who are committed to engaging in forms of development that challenge them to increase their self-awareness. Their numbers are expanding and include the visionaries and deep thinkers from all walks of life. Regardless of their professions, geographies, economic standing, political position, race, gender, or age, we want leaders that are centered in their beliefs and know themselves well enough to become the great leaders of tomorrow.

We can quickly discover those leaders who shy away from wanting to gain a deeper sense of self-awareness, those not willing to question their own actions and motives. They remain rigid, stuck in older ways of thinking, and continue to resist the changes knocking at their doors. They are the leaders who use conflict less as a constructive means to engage in collaboration and problem solving and more as ways through which to draw sides and polarize others. They work hard to hold on to assumptive beliefs and patterns of defensive behavior, while refusing to explore their behaviors, motivations, and the desires that reside at the core of their being.

Dedicating yourself to learning how to become a great leader will be one of the most difficult things you do in your life. Even when things look easy, you'll be surprised at how much you are being challenged to learn and grow. The greatest responsibility you will have is to explore yourself and apply what you learn to influence the world positively and constructively. To do so, you'll need to be honest with yourself, stripping away and casting aside all the ways in which you've learned to defend your failings and hide your flaws. Learning to become a true leader will require vulnerability and a willingness to understand yourself at the deepest levels imaginable. You will need to take risks not only in the world around you, but also with yourself, taking leaps of faith that you can trust in what is true about yourself.

There are no shortcuts to becoming a great leader. If you are in a leadership position, you've already realized this. Just because you are placed in a position of leadership or given the title doesn't make you a good leader. For most, this is the first signal that they better start learning. Once they take on the endeavor to educate themselves, they realize the significance of what they are being challenged to do. This is the sense every leader eventually gets, that although you will be asked to effectively manage conflict, you must confront your own internal struggles to succeed. You will have to take the journey to discover your unique and personal path to becoming a leader. And there are no shortcuts.

The Confidence to Lead

The only way to learn how to lead is through experience and a dedication to learning. Whether you see yourself as a natural born leader or a person who has learned the art of leadership through practical experience, leadership development, and training, you are learning as you go. Through my work, I've concluded that it is not one or the other; it is a combination of both. At the natural level, there will be aspects of your personality that lend themselves well to influencing others. At the learned level, your experiences in life will give you constant forms of feedback as to how you can use the traits and characteristics of your individuality to become an effective leader. Whether you consider yourself a born leader or someone learning to lead, you will always be a student of the art. Your experiences and perceptions of your successes and failures, and the stories you come to believe about yourself, will form your self-concept as a leader. The leader you want to be is a product of your own imagination, personality, and experiences.

This understanding is key to developing the interpersonal skills and confidence necessary for good leadership. Your experiences in life reveal what you are good at and what you are not good at. They form a construct for self-evaluation that you carry with you throughout your life, enabling you to become conscious and to think differently. Through this awareness, you are better able to lead more effectively.

The ways in which your perceived successes and failures influence you is incredibly powerful. This is likely not new to you. What is important is to recognize that the reason your experiences of success and failure are so significant and impactful is that they are all in some way related to conflict. Whether that conflict was with an individual, a group, or internal, it left an impression on you. The greater the emotional effect, the more likely you are carrying it with you as a permanent piece of your self-concept. This is especially true of traumatic conflicts that you carry in repressed or suppressed forms, unaware of their effect on your responses to high-stress situations. There are the big wins and big losses. There are the small wins and small losses. All are a part of who you are and influence the leader you wish to become.

In any situation, your confidence is the indicator of how good you feel about your chances of getting what you want. High self-confidence indicates that you anticipate success in achieving your goal. Low self-confidence reflects a fear that you'll not accomplish it. Your comfort in taking risks is also a reflection of this fear.

The lower your fear of failure, the safer you'll feel; the greater the predictability of success, the more confident you'll feel. Not every action you take will have a predictable outcome. This is a lesson you learned early in life. You have become an expert in effecting the predictability of your outcomes by being more aware of who you are. Your self-knowledge enables you to more consciously respond to the situations you find yourself in. This is particularly true in more difficult circumstances. Through better understanding yourself, you will become a more confident leader.

Your Life Story

I recently heard the accomplished author Stephen King talk about his approach to writing. The question of which characters he created are his favorites arose. He named a few that he was particularly fond of. He then explored the nature of fictional characters and how writers and readers connect to them. He spoke of the strong bonds that we can develop with characters within a story. This is the goal of writing a great story: creating characters that the reader will personally identify and connect with.

My experience with King led me to ask other writers about how they craft their stories. I learned that the basic ingredient to any story that captures our imagination is a great main character or group of central characters. Every story has four main ingredients: a context that provides the time, place, or setting; a central character or group of characters; a conflict; and a resolution. And though we might be disappointed at the end of the story if we don't like the resolution, we are even more disappointed when there is no clear ending. In such situations, we are dissatisfied at not having an outcome. Although we are more attracted to happy endings, it often doesn't matter whether the resolution is good or bad. We just want to know what happened to the main character.

You are the main character of your life story. As such, you store a host of memories that reflect the pleasant and unpleasant, happy and sad, successful and unsuccessful experiences of your life. Although you may not immediately recognize it, the majority of the key memories that you carry and are a part of your self-concept and beliefs stem from conflict. This includes how well you responded to and overcame them, as well as the mistakes you made along the way. They are also the experiences through which you develop the traits of your personality and patterns of behavior.

Many of the conflicts you engaged in occurred without your consciousness. Growing up, you likely encountered conflicts that presented themselves as consequences beyond your immediate control, moments in which you had neither the know-how nor wherewithal to respond. As a young child, in your adolescent years, and in young adulthood, you were engaged in relationships in which you felt helpless, had no recourse, had no voice, or no way out. You may have been ignored, bullied, ostracized, criticized, blamed, or emotionally and physically abused; all seemingly out of your control and often leaving you feeling like the victim. These experiences became a part of your life story. As the main character, they informed and shaped you, teaching you the ins and outs of conflict. Your experiences may have made you hard, tough, and a fighter. They may have left you fearful and withdrawn or perhaps over-accommodating to others and conflict avoidant. They may have left you numb to your emotions and feelings, a form of protection from the unpleasant or painful consequences and effects.

For example, for most of the first 30 years of my life, when it came to conflict, I was an expert avoider. That is not to say that I didn't like competition. I loved playing baseball, tennis, basketball, and soccer so much so that I was considered a standout player in each sport. On several occasions, until I graduated high school, I was chosen as team captain. I always had a hunger to be an accomplished performer and would spend long hours practicing and honing the skills I needed to perform well. In my young adulthood, at the Culinary Institute of America, I competed to be the best and won awards for my culinary skills. Unfortunately, like many people that have strong technical and business skills and can prove their worth through performing at high levels of competency, my competitive nature didn't always translate into strong conflict management skills.

Growing up, there were two forces that greatly influenced my beliefs about conflict. The first was my experience as an immigrant to the United States. I was four years old when my father brought my mother, my two brothers, and I to America. We crossed the Atlantic on the ocean liner SS Bremen, arriving at New York Harbor in 1961. Our first home was a small three-room apartment in Union City, New Jersey. At that time, the community just across the Hudson River from Manhattan was a wide-ranging blend of people from all ethnicities, heritages, religions, and cultures. Needless to say, fitting in was not always easy. As much as the community was vibrant and full of hope, it could also be uninviting, challenging, and scary. Not knowing any English and feeling like an outsider quickly made me a target of the other children. At school, to avoid being teased and threatened, I learned to keep to myself and limited my interactions with others. It wasn't until my family moved to a new home in the more accepting suburbs of northern New Jersey did I feel I could fit in. By then, I was entering third grade and began making friends in a new school and neighborhood where I felt much safer.[1]

The second great influence on my relationship to conflict was the modeling that shaped me at home. Being the youngest of three sons, I learned that it was best to avoid most of the conflict that came my way, especially when it had potentially physical consequences. In school and at home, the messages all reminded me to keep the peace, do what it takes to get along, and don't make other people angry.

As a child, my father grew up in the eastern part of Germany, a part of the country that at the end of World War II was annexed to Poland. He was 13 years old when the war came knocking at his family's door. One morning, the entire village was abruptly ordered to pack up what they could carry and forced from their homes. Shortly thereafter, my father was separated from his family. First mistreated by the Nazis and eventually taken by the enemy, he was imprisoned in a Russian camp. He underwent a great deal of emotional suffering, physical abuse, and psychological torture. He witnessed acts and crimes of war that deeply scarred his psyche and shaped his perception of human nature. Fearing that each day would be his last, he felt a complete loss of control.

Not too long ago, I asked him how he managed to deal with it. He told me it was difficult to explain. He said he went numb; that at times he disconnected himself to the point of not feeling his body any longer. He also learned to go emotionally silent, teaching himself not to feel his emotions. My father explained to me that the only thing left to think about was staying alive. To this day, he tells me that he is still not sure how he summoned the determination and resilience to stay alive. With a heavy shrug of his shoulders, he said: "That's all that was left." In his eyes I saw the distant and sorrowful look of a lost teenage boy.

After the war ended, he made his way back to the West, the main character in an incredible tale of resilience, strength, and remarkable ingenuity. Fighting starvation, he did whatever was necessary to find enough food to subsist on and, making his way through the war-ravished countryside that had been his home, deftly finding his way west to freedom. Years later, still heading west, he continued his journey and, as an immigrant in search of opportunity, brought his family to America.

My father's experiences left him deeply scarred. Though he was able to build a successful career and life for his family in America, he carried his experiences, trauma, and deep emotional scars with him. Like so many boys and young men, the experience of the war shaped his beliefs and attitude toward life and conflict. Similar to many people of his generation that experienced the darkest horrors of war, he was intensely affected.

Those who barely survived the ordeal as my father did typically dealt with it in one of three ways. Some learned to ignore their emotional pain and suffering, becoming numb to their anger and fear. They keep it deep within their souls, tucked away with the unimaginable, secretly breathing unspoken truths that silently haunt them, using assorted forms of escape to deaden their quiet suffering.

Others live with their unrelenting pain and, not confronting their demons, they wear their anger, living in fear and distrust, always furious with the world they see as letting them down, abandoning them in helpless suffering. They are the victims that make victims of others, finding outlets for their rage, targets for their anger, and moving in and out of the shadows of fear they cast on others.

The third group is made up of those who confront their anger and fear, deciding to talk about their experiences and finding pathways to the peace that they long for. They are the few that have discovered the power of accepting the past, discovering the powers of forgiveness and compassion, and using their experiences as energy and wisdom to create change. It takes courage to face the past, let go of anger, and tackle one's deep-seated fear. It requires one to have the courage to speak the truth. Embracing the truth and bringing it into the spoken realm is the most difficult undertaking of humanity.

For decades, my father fell into the second group. His defenses were driven by a fear of being hurt again. Like many people of his generation that lived through the horrific experience of war, he found it difficult to manage the psychological effects, including his anger, distrust, and blame. The greater the pain, the thicker the coat of armor one is capable of wearing. The greater the fear, the stronger your defenses become and the more you will practice and become versed at using them. My father's armor was thick and he became a master of defensiveness. In my own way, so did I.

As a young boy, I learned to avoid my father's anger and to not engage in any conflict with him. As a teenager, I became even better at it. By the time I graduated high school, I had become a full-blown expert at avoiding conflict or confronting the truth. It was not until I ventured into the world of psychology and studying leadership that I learned to leverage the power and wonderful outcomes that come from confronting conflict.

Years later, my father underwent a remarkable transformation. By confronting his internal conflicts and coming to terms with many of his experiences of war, he slowly began to let go of his old beliefs and became receptive to the new realities of his life. Through embracing his limiting and painful interpretations of his past, he rediscovered the young boy left behind five decades before. My father slowly came to realize the influence of his self-concept and, by becoming more aware, began to make the choices necessary to heal relationships and change his legacy. He has evolved into a loving man, adored by his grandchildren and great grandchildren, and admired by his friends.

In her wonderful book *Unbroken*, Laura Hillenbrand shares the remarkable story of Louis Zamperini, a World War II American pilot who, after his bomber crashes into the Pacific Ocean, survives one incredible ordeal after another. In describing Zamperini's resilience and survival at the hands of a brutal enemy officer while in captivity, Hillenbrand offers a powerful insight into the meaning of human dignity, describing it as essential to human life as water, food, and oxygen. She writes that "the stubborn retention of it, even in the face of extreme physical hardship, can hold a man's soul in his body long past the point at which the body should have surrendered it...without dignity, identity is erased."[2]

Unbroken is as much a great literary work as it is a remarkable story. Hillenbrand's portrayal of Louis Zamperini is a narrative guide to the brutal forms of behavior we engage in with one another. It also provides a wonderful insight into the astounding beauty of our ability to confront and overcome even the ugliest and most horrific aspects of conflict. When we uncover the resilience and innovation that conflict inspires, we get a glimpse into what is truly possible.

My father is a remarkable example of someone who was able to recover his identity and find his path to reclaiming his own sense of dignity. Through learning to confront his story of the past, he continues to grow more conscious of his role in his relationships and is reshaping the story of his life. He is building a legacy of a man not only of courage, strength, and immeasurable resilience, but also of a man who has rediscovered humanity and now lives a life of love and acceptance. And even though he has come a long way, he continues to learn and grow. It is something he is reminded of and continues to work on each and every day.[3]

The purpose of sharing my story is to give you a glimpse of how the relationships with our parents, families, and other significant people in our lives shape our self-concept and our individual perception of conflict. We all have our life story. Virtually all of us learned about conflict through our parents and families, which provided the life lessons and perceptions of ourselves that we carry throughout our lives. The more you understand what you learned and experienced, the more conscious you'll be of the choices you make. Without a doubt, at times this will be very hard work. At the same time, you'll find it well worth your effort. It is a daily undertaking. It is life.

Chapter Summary

⫽ A leader's self-awareness has become the most critical aspect of leadership.

⫽ We can quickly spot leaders who avoid searching for a deeper sense of self, those who are unwilling to question their actions and motives. They remain rigid, stuck in older ways of thinking, and resist change.

⫽ Learning to become a true leader will require vulnerability and a willingness to understand yourself at the deepest levels possible.

⫽ Your experiences in life provide insight on how to use the traits and characteristics of your individuality to become a more effective leader.

Chapter 9

SELF-INVENTION

All your life you've been inventing who you are and the person you want to be. As the main character in your own life story, your self-concept is the expression of your life and how your experiences have shaped and guided you. In essence, all your life you've been evolving your self-concept: the social, physical, emotional, and spiritual perception you have of yourself. Ever since you were a young child, you've been receiving feedback from the world around you. You decide whether the reaction to your behavior is what you want and whether it feels good or not. You are constantly evaluating the responses you get, seeking to understand what it says about who are.

Your journey to leadership asks that you self-invent to become the ideal you. The input you receive indicates if you are succeeding and lets you know if your behavior is acceptable or not. It also let's you know whether you're living up to the image of yourself that

Self-Invention

you portray to the world. The resulting feedback forms your core beliefs.

Beginning with your parents, all your life you've been influenced by feedback from others. Your external experience and relationships to others informs your internal experience. Those experiences eventually influence the beliefs you hold about yourself. During your younger years, you didn't question the views others had of you, nor did you question their sources.

What you did pay particular attention to were the responses to your behaviors from your parents and immediate family members.[1] Eventually, this included other authority figures such as your teachers and coaches. Your friends also became a part of the group of people who had a great influence on your life and whose opinions still matter most. The more significant people are to you, the more likely you are to be swayed by their views. This is a reminder that everything is personal. You take all the feedback as inputs into how you will get what you want and what will make you happier and more satisfied with your self-concept.

As a leader, you realize that the number of those willing to give you feedback increases. There are many people you know (and even some you may never meet) who are willing to give you their opinions, criticisms, and advice. This not only broadens and increases the amount of feedback, but also heightens its influence on you and your self-concept.

Your social perception is the result of the core beliefs you have about how you fit in and what your place is with others. It informs how you believe you are welcome and asked to participate with others, how you feel included, where you fit into the social hierarchy, and how much you can afford to show of your genuine self. Like everyone, you have some desire to feel like you belong, that you are significant, and that others are willing to pay attention to you and invite you into the group or community you long to be a member of.

As a leader, you also want to know your place in the hierarchy. You accomplish this by demonstrating your abilities, competencies, and knowledge to everyone. The "social pecking order" reflects one's level of achievement, the social influence one gains through being competent and competing well, and the status achieved from it.

Your social perception also informs how open and expressive you can be with others. As I mentioned earlier, how accepted we feel by others allows us to judge how much we can share of what we think, see, and feel. In any social setting, your discernment of acceptance for who you really are guides how open you can be without the risk of being socially rejected and, thus, excluded or ostracized.

Your physical self-perception informs how good you feel about your appearance and bodily health. Everyone concerns themselves with their appearance. Your perceptions about your height, weight, sexuality, race, attractiveness, and age are some of the more common factors that decide how happy you are with your physical being. The reason you look into the mirror in the morning is to evaluate whether your appearance best expresses who you are and whether you are happy with how you look. You do this to predict how others will respond to your appearance. There are deep core beliefs about your self that stem from your physical self-concept. Again, these beliefs are products of the feedback you've received throughout your life.

One of the first lessons we learn as children is that appearances matter. You learn quickly that your appearance has a tremendous effect on how others perceive you. When we realize the influence our self-concept has on our self-esteem, we can hardly blame people for being over-concerned about their appearance. Additionally, the emphasis society places on how people look gives us a great deal of insight and understanding into why some are considered vain.

The messages you receive about your physical self-concept come not only from the outside, but are also manifestations of how healthy you feel physically. Your level of energy, your awareness of your stress levels, and your physical responses to conflict are all aspects of your perceptions of your body. I find this aspect of one's self-concept to be of particular value to leaders. How you feel and carry yourself, and how relaxed and physically confident you are influences others.

Though many leaders put on appearances, there is a great deal of trust conveyed through the ability to be authentic. After all, one aspect of your appearance that is difficult to alter and has a priceless influence is the look in your eyes. If your eyes are the windows through which to see the real you, it is always a good idea to know how you are feeling. So much of who you are and your present emotional state is conveyed through your eyes. Never underestimate this aspect of your appearance. Regardless of what you do with the rest of your appearance, others will always see the truth in your eyes.

When it comes to aging, there are tradeoffs. On one hand, it's good to feel and appear young and strong, but on the other hand, showing emotional maturity and wisdom benefits looking your age, especially when making the shift to middle age. In the end, it's up to you to decide. What is certain is that, like everyone, you will undergo the internal conflicts of aging. I therefore suggest you get ready for it and leverage it when it happens.

Your emotional self-concept is your perception of how happy you are. As a leader, you will always strive to be better at what you do and how you do it. Based on your outcomes, you will judge yourself on a spectrum ranging from satisfaction to dissatisfaction on whether or not you are living up to your ideal self. Though your level of happiness and contentment has much to do with how you perceive your present situation, it also informs how you believe your actions and outcomes align with your legacy. This is true even if you are operating at only a surface level of awareness. Your emotional being provides you the capability to be more aware. This is a key element of your self-awareness: your ability to recognize in the moment how you are responding emotionally. When you are feeling happy, you are generally getting your desires and needs met. When you are feeling unhappy, it is because the opposite is occurring. When you are unhappy you may not only experience melancholy, sadness, and disappointment, but also may find yourself in the role of the victim, blaming everyone and everything around you for getting in the way of your happiness. Eventually, your misery will lead to feelings of hopelessness. Or, your discontent becomes resentment and anger, which you take out on others. The deeper and more hidden your anger, the more likely you will engage in patterns of dysfunctional behavior with others. As the old saying goes, you are angry at the world and you go home and take it out on the dog.

Eventually, being unconscious of your emotional self-concept results in suppressing or ignoring your feelings and leaving you unaware of how you are acting out your dissatisfaction. Furthermore, you won't recognize the internal conflicts that motivate your behavior. As a leader, therefore, awareness of your emotional satisfaction is a valuable asset. As we will discuss later, the path to exploring your behavior begins with the ability to be present and aware of your emotions. This will enable you to be more aware of your emotional self-concept, thereby allowing you to choose the strategies and behaviors that will lead to higher levels of contentment.

Every person desires to feel happy. In light of this, it is natural for you to find the shortest and fasted route to happiness. Like most, you'll find that happiness is much less the sense of an immediate accomplishment than it is a consequence of doing those things that make you feel happy. Martin Seligman, a University of Pennsylvania psychologist who in 1998 coined the term "positive psychology," provided some of the best insights on happiness. Seligman said that happiness is the result of experiencing pleasure from things around us without making them our primary focus. As a leader, this notion is key to how you relate to happiness and a measurement of how happy you feel.

Leaders typically show a strong tendency to try to accomplish higher level goals and outcomes. The belief is that once they attain the goal, they will be happy. As you have likely already discovered, this is typically a short-lived state of contentment. I have found this experience to be common among leaders. As a leader, you are likely to experience the joy of your accomplishments for short periods and then find yourself impatient and ready for your next challenge.

The lasting and memorable sources of happiness are not to be found in the end result but, rather, in the journey. True feelings of happiness are experienced when one is feeling fully engaged in a challenging activity, building significant relationships with others, or doing something that brings meaning to one's life. Much like building your legacy, your happiness is derived from doing all the things that get you there.

This is why we often see leaders who are never truly happy with their achieved goals. As soon as the goals are reached, they begin to define and chase new ones. With time, they are dissatisfied with their lives; they feel they are missing something and are still seeking happiness. Knowing this shows that the happiness which results from being mindful and aware of your experience provides you with a greater sense of long-term well-being.

Your happiness is not derived from the attainment of an outcome, but rather is the result of the experience and meaning gained from fulfilling it. In material terms, happiness comes not from belongings and money, but from what they represent. The possessions are your evidence and provide you, and the world around you, with a scorecard to how well you're doing in satisfying your self-concept.

A great example of this approach to thinking about happiness is Warren Buffet. Nicknamed "The Sage of Omaha" for his investment and business capabilities, Buffet consistently ranks as one of the wealthiest people in the world. In February of 2015, in a meeting with students of the Ivey Business School, he was asked to define success and how this definition had changed through the course of his career. This is how he responded:

> The saying goes that success is about getting what you want, while happiness is about wanting what you get. For myself, happiness is more important. My goal was always financial independence; working for myself and finding a job where I admire the people I work with. I was interested in being in a position to control the decision-making process. At age 25, I had enough money to live off of. I had two children and the equivalent of roughly $2 million in today's money. Everything since then has been surplus.
>
> As you move along in your career, you always want to consider your inner scorecard—how you feel about your own performance and success. You should worry more about how well you perform rather than how well the rest of the world perceives your performance. The success of Berkshire has always been more important than my own personal success in terms of financial returns. The most important takeaway is that you should always try to be a good person.[2]

Despite all the accolades, material evidence, and self-assurance of success, it always comes back to your understanding of yourself and your relationship with the world.

The fourth element of your self-concept is your spiritual percep-tion. This is the way in which you see your connection to a greater being or nature, and shapes the core values that you strive to live up to. Whether it is through a form of religion, a metaphysical source, nature, a holy pursuit, or a belief in a mystical source of energy, your spiritualty provides you with a sense of connection to some-thing or someone beyond your physical self. For most people, their spiritual perception is an indication of their faith in, and relation-ship to, a greater power. God, Mother Nature, and other forms and figures also create a connection to other people and communities that share the same set of beliefs and values.

Beyond connecting to a source of greater power, this element of your self-concept is a powerful reflection of how well you are living up to the standards and models of behavior that your reli-gious viewpoint or spiritual philosophy provides. More than rules, your spirituality is the source of the core values that manifest your moral and ethical principles. It is through this lens that you judge to what extent your thoughts and actions are virtuous, decent, up-right, and respectable. To a great degree, your sense of morality and your self-worth reflect how well you live up to the standards of your values.

In my experience, most leaders desire to be admired by oth-ers. Although others' admiration can be based on your competen-cy and accomplishments, at a deeper level it is a confirmation of how they perceive your alignment with the values and beliefs you espouse. This is an indicator of how others see you as authentic, honest, and forthright and how well your behavior toward them is aligned with your intention.

As a leader, it is important that you develop a commitment to live in alignment with your values. It isn't always necessary that others agree with you. What is important is that they see who you are and that you are transparent in your beliefs. The result will be a greater trust in your leadership and you as a person.

Experiences, Feedback, and Beliefs

Throughout your life you naturally create the person you want to be. You inherently strive to live up to your ideal self-image, which you continuously shape and refine. The closer you move toward the ideal self, the better and more content you feel. The greater the gap between your real self and your ideal self, the less secure and confident you are, the greater your dissatisfaction. You think to yourself, "I should be doing this differently" or evaluate what you've done with "I should have..." statements, thinking that you are failing to live up to your own standards. This reveals an internal conflict because of the gap between what you're getting and what you want.

You're always judging yourself and determining whether you're getting what you want. Throughout your life, from the moment you came into the world, you have ongoing experiences that provide you with insight and feedback that become a part of your self-concept. Because conflict is central to your experiences, the moments in which you underwent more intense conflict—and because of the emotions that accompany them—become the key sources of feedback that form your core beliefs.

Your beliefs about how smart, lovable, competent, important, brave, or weak you are reflect the judgments you are making about yourself. One of the great fallacies is the one that states, "I can be nonjudgmental." When you make this comment, it is evident that you're already judging yourself. It's natural to judge, to be critical of our own actions. Further, I would suggest that the ability to recognize when you are judging yourself is a powerful aspect of self-awareness. When you're judging, it's a sign that you're determining whether or not you are living up to your ideals. Doing so can provide you with powerful insights about yourself and connect you to the sources of your emotion.

Values, Beliefs, and an Open Mind

Your life story is the source of your values and core beliefs that mold and influence the views and assumptions you make about yourself as a leader. The less aware you are of your values and core beliefs, the more likely you are to make false assumptions about your influence and about your relationships. The more you choose to ignore the feedback the world offers, the more likely you will find yourself in conflict with others.

Having an open mind and a willingness to explore the opinions and viewpoints of others is an important capability to develop. There are multiple benefits that you will receive. For starters, by exploring the response you get to your behaviors, you can search whether your behavior is consistent with your intentions. If you're missing the mark, a good place to start is by assessing your behavior. Great leaders come to terms with the responsibility they have by assuring that their behavior and their communication is aligned with their intention.

A second benefit is the increased understanding of your defensive triggers. It is important to continuously learn about what solicits your defensive responses. Whenever you get triggered, you have to ask yourself what you are emotionally responding to. Your defenses are the ways in which you play out the fears of not attaining your desired self-concept. The internal conflicts and issues that you carry become your triggers. For example, I schedule a meeting for my team. It's well past the starting time and two members of the team have not yet arrived. The assumption I make is that they do not see me as important enough and, by not attending, they are ignoring me. My self-concept is telling me that they are discounting my leadership. The origin of my true fear is that I am not as significant as I should be and, therefore, people will not pay enough attention for me to be successful.

A third benefit is that when you become more aware of your own fear, you can choose your behavior more effectively. Rather than blaming others, you can confront your internal fear and become more open-minded as to what is actually happening. In the previous example, what leads me to believe that members of my team are intentionally late is the expression of my own fear. Through being aware of my fear, I can embrace it, move past it, and then let go of the story. Rather than let it consume my thoughts and energy, and perhaps blame others, I can now focus on the meeting in a more constructive manner to attain my desired outcomes.

Another outcome of my increased awareness is dealing with others more effectively and with greater openness and acceptance of who they are and what their circumstances are. The team members are very likely already concerned about their late arrival. My ability to be open to their circumstance and concern not only helps them, it also increases my self-concept and image as a leader. When the members of the team finally arrive, rather than criticize them and risk putting them in a defensive position, I can simply inquire what led to their late arrival.

Your ability to be present and self-aware results in feeling "centered." This is a trait that carries with it the sense of confidence that will give others a sense of security. There is calmness that typically accompanies a leader who exhibits this form of emotional awareness. The more self-aware you are, the more likely others will see you as thoughtful and patient.

As a leader, one of the most important aspects of your development is understanding your behavior. Is it all about you? Yes it is. To confront conflict requires a desire for openness to self-knowledge. If you are closed and cut off the flow of feedback from others, you can easily become egotistical, self-deceptive, and fall victim to your own fears. Rather than confront and constructively leverage your internal conflicts, you will succumb to them.

To be successful requires you to become intimate with who you are and embrace your self-concept. The willingness to be open to yourself is the first step in inviting others to be open with you, to see you as approachable, so they can trust that you will be open to their thoughts, viewpoints, opinions, and ideas. It is important to be aware of the four levels required to be a great leader: the global, the organizational, the interpersonal, and the self. As you will inevitably learn, the most important of these is the self. It is the source of your power of choice.

Chapter Summary

⚏ All your life you've been inventing who you are and the person you want to be.

⚏ As the main character in your life story, your self-concept is the expression of your life and how your experiences have shaped and guided you.

⚏ Beginning with your parents, you've been influenced by the feedback you get, which eventually forms the beliefs you hold about yourself.

⚏ As a leader, you quickly realize that the number of those willing to give you feedback increases.

⚏ Your happiness is not derived from attaining outcomes, but from the experience of fulfilling them.

⚏ Having an open mind and a willingness to explore the opinions and viewpoints of others is an important capability to develop.

⚏ A valuable outcome of your increased awareness is the ability to deal with others more effectively.

⚏ It is important to be aware of the four levels required to be a great leader: the global, the organizational, the interpersonal, and the self.

Chapter 10

THE HOLY GRAIL OF LEADERSHIP

The most important skill you will need to develop to become a great leader is the ability to understand your behavior. Throughout my study and coaching of leaders, I have come to realize this to be the holy grail of leadership. There is nothing more powerful than understanding your behavior and realizing the power to consciously choose what you do and say. It is the core characteristic and skill of leadership greatness.

When it comes to engaging in conflict, there's hardly a leader that won't try to win. I've not yet met one that isn't interested in getting what they want or not willing to compete to get it. That's one of the core characteristics that all leaders have in common. Even in situations in which leaders are engaging conflict in collaborative ways and problem solving with others, they will in some shape or form be looking out for their own interest or gain. Then again, we all do. Leaders just make a habit of doing it better than others. And, because they are typically good at it, others will rely on the leader to also get them what they are looking for. That's what attracts many to the leaders they follow. It's also what attracts you to wanting to lead.

As a leader, there is a spectrum of behaviors that you can employ to engage in conflict. The primary forms include avoidance, competing to win, negotiating a compromise, and problem solving. You can also try to understand what the other party wants and work toward meeting their desired outcome. Whether you end up collaborating, compromising, or accommodating others, don't be surprised to find yourself bargaining to get something in return. Even the most altruistic of intentions provides you with some form of return, including admiration for your good intentions and deeds.

The same can be said when you comply with the requests or demands of someone you are in conflict with. Though you may find it worthwhile to agree with needs of the other party, at some level you are seeking to fulfill one of your needs. Conceding and accommodating are often ways of managing conflict through avoidance. Although you may see giving in to the other party as noble on your part, most of the time you'll find that you have an underlying motivation to obliging, cooperating with, or accommodating another person's desired outcome. Getting along with others can also lead to people admiring you because they see your actions as unselfish and in the service to others. As we all know, the need to be loved is a powerful motivator.

More often than not, the patterns of behavior that leaders engage in reflect their desire to achieve a benefit. If you find yourself doing the same thing, don't be overly alarmed; it's what is expected of you. It is normal that others expect you to find a path to winning and to influence them in joining you. It's worth reminding yourself that, if it were not for conflict, you would likely not be needed by others to lead. It's how you go about it that matters so much.

Like many leaders, this is where you may find yourself at a crossroads. If you are aware, you will discover that you have the choice to simply do what you always do while uncovering other options. Rather than being subject to your patterns, you discover that you have options as to how you confront conflict and, in turn, how you want to lead.

The Ultimate Skill

As a leader, the key skill that you must have to reach your peak level of performance is understanding your own behavior. This level of self-awareness is not easy to attain. (If it were, you would likely not be reading this book.) It is hard work and demands a great deal of dedication and inner strength. Yet every step on your path of self-discovery will be worth it regardless of how difficult it may appear. As I mentioned earlier, the intimate relationship between creating change, confronting conflict, and self-knowledge is undeniable. In the end, the key to successfully managing and leveraging it is how well you know yourself.

I often get asked by leaders to help them build and hone their communication and conflict management skills. At the surface level, the vast majority of leaders are seeking techniques and step-by-step approaches to being more effective. Though these are certainly worthwhile and offer a great deal of value, your ability to successfully apply any methodology is dependent on acting consciously. Ultimately, managing your relationships relies on having the presence of mind to effectively employ a method when needed. This is particularly true when you are under a great deal of stress. There's plenty of anxiety, tension, and urgency that the demands of leadership will provoke. Inevitably, the pressure you are under will stir up your emotions and take you down the path of either confronting your fear or falling prey to it. If you don't face your inner conflicts, sooner or later you'll find yourself in unproductive and defensive patterns of avoidance and dysfunction. When this happens, it becomes difficult to apply any methodology, regardless of how good it is.

Self-knowledge is more than an element of great leadership; it is a necessity. Fortunately, it is a conscious competency that you can attain. Virtually every human being has the ability to learn about themselves. Even though it is likely that you will never truly master it, this journey will prove to be the most important undertaking of your life. It's worth repeating that it will not be easy. Then again, the most important challenges—those that are truly worth striving for and which provide the greatest rewards—rarely are.

The Four Beliefs

There are times when you are unconscious of your beliefs, of the assumptions about yourself, and of attitudes and self-perceptions that are the products of your upbringing and experiences. Often, until you are in a situation that forces you to become aware of your beliefs, you can remain unconscious of them. The means through which you become more aware of your beliefs is through better understanding your behavior.

There are four beliefs about yourself that are critical to your self-concept and that are necessary to adopt and develop in order to succeed. Becoming aware of, embracing, and consciously developing these beliefs will directly improve the quality of your leadership and increase your confidence as a leader. They are:

- "I am capable of emotional awareness."
- "I have the power to choose my behavior."
- "I am open to understanding others."
- "I can change how I feel about myself."

Together, these four beliefs provide a rich framework for the self-knowledge and awareness required to become a leader who is capable of managing and using conflict effectively.

"I am capable of emotional awareness."

When you become more observant and better understand your behavior, you will be able to explore the emotions behind what you do and say. As a result, you will also better distinguish the variety of emotions you engage in. Happiness, sadness, confidence, angst, enthusiasm, determination, and compassion are all examples of the array of emotions you are capable of expressing. The more you are in touch with your emotions, the better you will be able to link them to your desires and needs. The more you do this, the more you become intimate with your self-concept—the social, physical, emotional, and spiritual perception you hold of yourself.

You will also become versed in understanding the intensity of your emotions. Often, you'll find that you can keep an emotion under check while paying little attention to it. This doesn't always coincide with the intensity that it carries. Being more emotionally aware will not only attune you to the apparent emotions, but also to those below the surface. For example, one of your colleagues repeatedly ignores your requests for information. Each time it happens, you feel slighted. One day, he does it again. This time, rather than just keeping your feelings to yourself, you storm into his office yelling and questioning what is wrong with him.

Often, in working with leaders, I have found that they can become comfortable with a negative emotion and come to consider it as part of the job. "It comes with the territory" is the old and familiar adage. Another is, "They don't have to like me. They just have to respect me." There are dangers that come with this mindset. For one, if the emotion is negative and persistent, it can wear you down and create ripple effects including problems with health and relationships. Secondly, because of your desire to be combative, you can actually become addicted to it. Whether you consider it an external conflict or an unreconciled issue within yourself, you may be feeding it by avoiding its cause. Much like playing the part of the victim, you can also play the hero to fulfill a need for attention. You can find yourself creating crisis after crisis that only you can fix. In doing so, you are encouraging a dysfunctional pattern of behavior to take hold in your relationships, as well as in the culture of the team and organization you lead.

"I have the power to choose my behavior."

By being self-aware and understanding your behavior, you come to realize that you are in control of everything you do and say. Therefore, if you have the desire or need to, you can choose to change your behavior. The most powerful thing in your life is the power of choice. From one moment to the next, you can change your behavior and thus immediately change your influence others. It then stands to reason that there is no more powerful skill than the ability to be aware of your emotions.

This is key to understanding yourself as a leader. The very definition of leadership is influencing others to act. To influence others to take action and respond to your leadership requires an awareness of your current behavior. If you're not getting the result you want, the only way to change this result is to change your behavior. This belief is key to influencing others to respond to you in a manner that best contributes to fulfilling your goals.

"I am open to understanding others."

This is the belief that understanding your own behavior increases your ability to be open to and better understand the behavior of others. When you recognize that your behavior is an expression of your feelings, emotions, and needs, you become more open to understanding the behavior and emotion of others. I am not suggesting that you have to accept the behavior of others, especially when they are not aligned with the core values of your culture. I am advocating that if you are open to understanding the behavior of others, you will greatly benefit as a leader. You will learn more about others and yourself.

When you find yourself in a conflict situation, your first response reflects a tendency to focus on yourself. Getting your own needs met will almost always guide your first response. In light of this, your inclination will be to make assumptions about the other person's behavior and the threat they might pose to you. You are reacting from a predisposition to your fears, using blame, criticism, threat, and a host of other behaviors as a defense. None of these tactics and behaviors will serve the purpose of listening to or understanding the other person's point of view.

As the result of becoming more self-aware, you will learn how to not always rely on or immediately respond through your defensive patterns and assumptions, increasing your ability to understand our differences. We are all owners of our emotions, needs, and desires. It is important to recognize how powerful it is to understanding the behaviors of others. Not only will you become more knowledgeable of the motivations of those you are in conflict with, you will also be testing your own assumptions and challenging yourself to attain deeper levels of self-knowledge.

"I can change how I feel about myself."

The fourth belief is that through your ability to recognize the origin of your feelings, you can change your self-concept. With this belief you can acknowledge that you don't have to accept the assumptions about yourself. You don't have to accept the idea that you need to continue wearing the same masks and personas you've invented. You don't have to continue engaging in patterns of behavior that are misaligned with who you want to be or no longer reflect the true you.

There is a rich and deeply rewarding experience that results from the ability to connect your emotions to your self-concept. Because your self-concept is home to the beliefs you hold about yourself, it is also the part of your being that governs your ability for intimacy and vulnerability. Your self-concept is the source of your desire for love, self-worth, success, and the core values you strive to live through. As you peel away the layers of your emotions, you inevitably come to the place where the true you resides. Your self-concept is where you store and hold the beliefs that define the true you.

Your self-esteem reflects whether you are living up to the expectations that define your ideal self. When your needs are being met, you feel good about yourself and have high self-esteem. When your needs are not being met, you feel less content and have low self-esteem.

When you have low self-esteem, you are likely to feel insecure and be in conflict with others. In particular, you'll likely find yourself in conflict with those people that you hold responsible for getting in the way of meeting your needs. Because they are interfering with your goals you hold them responsible for the way you feel.

When you make others responsible for your feelings, you miss the opportunity to explore your beliefs about who you are and how you feel about yourself. Through exploring your beliefs as the source of your feelings you can make more conscious choices about which beliefs represent who you really are. Perhaps they are the result of experiences in your life and messages others provided about your failures. Or they are beliefs that at some point you decided to keep alive to please someone or fit in with others. It could be a false belief you held on to in order to win a parent's love or approval.

Creating this level of awareness will not come without its share of emotional trials and challenges. What I can tell you is that it will be worth it. For when you let go of old, untrue, and limiting beliefs, you will change the way you feel. You will feel at ease and more confident. You will be more authentic and truthful in your relationships. What will emerge is a strengthened source of influence and leadership. You will find that changing the way you feel about yourself will directly improve your ability to manage and use conflict more effectively.

The Power of Choice

The better you understand your behavior, the more you will be present and attentive to the moment. This is the result of your emotions and actions being less influenced by fear. It is an outcome you are creating by being emotionally aware, open to others, and living and acting in alignment with your core values and beliefs.

As a leader, others expect that you will be conscious of your behavior, especially in situations of conflict. They will expect you to stay in control of your actions. They look to you to make the choices that best respond to the moment at hand. When it comes to conflict, they want and need you to be effective. They need to be secure in knowing that you will be in control of your emotions and respond constructively. As human beings, we all want a sense of predictability and security.

Having emotional awareness and believing in yourself will allow you to leverage the most powerful aspect of your behavior: choice. As we will explore in the following chapter, how you use your power to consciously choose your behavior will determine how you'll improve in managing and using conflict. It is the difference between being rigid and stuck in your current patterns of behavior, or becoming more adaptable and flexible, thus finding new paths to becoming a great leader.

Chapter Summary

⟋ Self-knowledge is more than an element of great leadership; it is a necessity.

⟋ There are four beliefs that are critical to your self-concept and that are necessary for you to succeed.

⟋ When you become more observant and better understand your behavior, you will be able to explore the emotions behind what you do and say.

⟋ By being self-aware and understanding your behavior, you come to realize that you are in control of everything you do and say.

⟋ The most powerful thing you have in your life is the power of choice.

⟋ When you become more aware of your behavior, you become more open to understanding the behavior of others.

⟋ Through recognizing the origins of your feelings, you can change your self-concept.

⟋ Your power of choice is the difference between being rigid and stuck in current patterns of behavior, and becoming adaptable and finding new paths to becoming a great leader.

Chapter 11

THE LURE OF AVOIDANCE

If you are going to be a good role model and lead by example, you will have to get comfortable with confronting conflict. The problem is that as much as leaders express their discomfort with conflict, they are even more averse to confronting it. For this reason, it's a good idea to understand that there is a distinct difference between confronting a conflict and being directly engaged in it.

The word "confront" can conjure up a host of definitions and interpretations. As with anything in life, your understanding of this word results from your experiences of being confronted and confronting others. When most people think about confronting another person, they typically think about a face-to-face argument or a fight of some kind.[1] This means that aggression is involved and that there will be a loser and a winner. A win or lose attitude naturally evokes all the fears that you may have about conflict and how successfully you face it. This perspective to confrontation might emphasize the importance of winning or compel you to consider avoiding conflict altogether.

I strongly suggest that you broaden your definition of the word "confront," recognizing its more positive and constructive meaning. By doing so, you become more conscious of your choices and much more effective. Let's start with the full definition of the word.

At its root, the word "confront" means to face something. The act of confronting is facing and dealing with a problem or difficult situation. To become more familiar with the constructive and positive aspect of this word, here are some synonymous meanings:

- To address.
- To come to grips with.
- To tackle.
- To see to.
- To grapple with.
- To deal with.
- To handle.
- To attend to.
- To manage.

To this list, I suggest you add "to lead."

The definition I like to use when coaching leaders and in my workshops is "to face the truth." Rather than thinking of conflict as a form of separation and a means to hostility and combativeness, I suggest you think of it as an invitation to the party you are in conflict with, asking them to participate in exploring the real issues and challenges that need to be discussed.

To succeed in encouraging others to play differently demands a significant shift in your thinking. Based on your experiences and learning, you might assume that others are apt to be aggressive during conflict and, therefore, you must counter forcefully. Consciously changing your thinking means using confrontation as a path to a more collaborative dialogue. However, a conversation that is more problem-centered will likely require you to confront your own beliefs about the use of strength and ideology.

When thinking about the more constructive and positive view of confrontation, you will also find it useful identifying and coming to terms with the various forms of avoidance you may be using. Avoidance is a tempting proposition. Yet, if your aim is to lead an innovative and open culture, there is no room for it.

The Art of Avoidance

Whether one is responding to fear, anger, or another form of anxiety, avoidance of conflict is one of the most common approaches to conflict that leaders take. By avoiding conflict, you'll find that you are either feeding the elephant or that you've taken the role of the biggest elephant. Often, leaders that avoid conflict are not fully aware that they are doing it. Because our interpretations of conflict come from conscious and unconscious beliefs, it feels safer to avoid conflict than to confront it.

It is important to recognize that your beliefs are expressions of your desires and needs, and are the origins of your emotions. Due to the flight or fight instinct, it feels safer to avoid the conflict, regardless of how small or big it may be or how conscious you are of it. Out of sight and out of mind is a frequent hope that leaders have.

In the previous chapter, I described how your self-concept is influenced by your experiences, values, core beliefs, and emotional desires and needs. It is the latter of these, your desires and needs, which allow us to better understand the most frequent reasons that leaders avoid conflict. At a deeper level, the fear of being incompetent results in feelings of embarrassment and humiliation. The fear of not being liked and loved for your actions results in feeling rejected and unloved.

The lack of confrontation acts as a defense to being seen as incompetent and rejected and can result in several forms of avoidance, none of which are aligned with great leadership. The following are some examples of avoidance that you may employ as a result. I also include suggestions on taking action to avoid falling into the negative consequences of these different avoidance tactics.

⫽ *Shifting responsibility* and indirectly expecting someone else to take care of it. Much like "passing of the buck," this approach to avoidance makes someone else responsible for confronting and managing the conflict. When you engage in this form of avoidance, you can then expect others to do the same; hence the problems continuously flow downhill, spreading to more and more people. Sooner or later, the conflict finds its way to people who don't know what they are supposed to do, don't feel empowered to act, and are left wondering why leadership hasn't done anything. Eventually, your blame of others will find its way back to you.

Suggestion: first, begin with becoming aware of your patterns of shifting responsibility and then stop when you discover yourself doing it. The second step is to make others aware of the responsibility that they have to not engage in the same form of avoidance. By doing so, you are communicating the importance of your expectations for how conflict is managed in your culture. Lastly, ask others to let everyone know when someone is shifting responsibility. It's a good practice to actively check with others and ask for feedback. Realizing the power that comes from your role modeling, it may take some courage to ask others to remind you when you are not aligned with your own expectations. It will require even more courage to be open to the answer.

⫽ *Denying* that a conflict exists. This form of avoidance also leads to downplaying or smoothing over conflict. From "What elephant?" you modify your approach to "Oh, that little elephant? It will go away. It's not a big enough animal to even consider worrying about." Just don't be surprised if the little elephant starts following you around. Denial can also be an unconscious act of avoidance.

Suggestion: pay attention to your thoughts and notice when you shift away from thinking about a conflict or how effectively you devalue it. This is not as easy as it sounds and takes practice. Another strategy is to ask those around you to bring any conflict in your organization, team, or with you to your attention. Your ability to listen and respond will be the best form of encouragement you can offer. It's easy to fall into patterns of denial, especially if you've already been doing it. When you get the help of others, realize that they too are changing their behavior. Remember to say "thank you" and show your gratitude and appreciation for their efforts.

Confusion, chaos, and the circumstances of change all provide fertile ground for avoidant behavior. You may find yourself relying on the explanation that the conflict is a result of the confusion and chaos people are working in. You can also find yourself employing misdirection here, using this explanation as a distraction that will eventually take care of itself. You believe that, because the conflict arose out of chaos, as soon as things settle down it will go away. In some circumstances this may be true. It's also true that there are chances for problem solving, creating improvements, and other opportunities for innovation that will be missed.

Suggestion: even if it's too much to ask to confront every opportunity, you are responsible for paying close attention, identifying the opportunities, and prioritizing and acting on those that will provide you with benefit. Along the way, you are teaching others that often the best innovations are discovered in moments of chaos and confusion. You will learn that even in chaos and confusion there are patterns of behavior that emerge. The patterns provide some consistencies to environments in which people fear a loss of control. Unfortunately, much like when people during times of change don't have information and turn to making up stories, the same holds true for conflict. It is the same thread of cause and effect. Therefore, your inaction and avoidance will only fuel the fires of unproductive conflict. When there is chaos, confusion, and change, take the time to talk to people, actively engaging them in spotting the elephants. Not only will you be confronting real issues, you'll also find what information people need and will help them to avoid the rumor mill and unproductive conflict.

⫸ *Hesitation* can deliver both short- and long-term avoidance. Caused by fear, self-doubt, or the lack of belief in your capability to manage it effectively, you may hesitate to confront the conflict in the present. Unfortunately, hesitation often leads to procrastination, which results in continued avoidance.

Suggestion: when you find yourself waffling, stop what you're doing, assess your behavior, consciously sort your fears, and create a plan to confront the situation. Often, I find this to be a good opportunity to engage others to participate and collaborate with you. Once you talk about it, you discover the truth and create a public commitment to take action.

⫸ *Skepticism* is a form of avoidance that places fault on others. As a leader, you claim that your inability to confront conflict is the result of the organization's or team's culture. Take caution here, as your cynicism can undermine anyone's ability to voice even the most important of matters. If you don't care, why should they?

Suggestion: it is important that you avoid this form of blaming others. If you are being skeptical, stop and explore the causes of your own distrust in the culture. When you do so, you will likely find different reasons for your lack of faith. And when you do, rather than claim everyone else is letting you down, take action and engage others to reset expectations, clearly communicating how you want to use and manage conflict going forward. In the end, it will take less energy than is being consumed chasing and cleaning up the messes created by avoidance—energy that can be better applied to creating positive change.

Keeping the peace will not only support your desire for harmony, it will also make you feel like one of the team. Whether it feeds a desire for inclusion or saves you from being disliked, because you fear raising an issue and rocking the boat, you are contributing to a fake reality that everything is alright. A false truce never solves the problem at hand. The bigger elephant in the boat that will eventually sink you is constant compromise. When a culture falls into consistent forms of compromise, people find temporary solutions and the root causes of conflict are never dealt with. Much like a bad marriage, people will learn to live with unresolved issues and, with time, come to be resentful and act out their discontent in dysfunctional ways.

Suggestion: first and foremost, become aware of when you're participating in bargaining that leads to peacekeeping and compromise. Identify what matters to you most and why there is a conflict in the first place. Then find a way to communicate it. It's important to speak out on what matters to you most, letting others know of the problem that needs to be dealt with. Doing so also allows you to focus more on the problem and less on your fear. A deeper issue that you'll be dealing with is not allowing a compromise to affect the core values of your culture. When you compromise and avoid conflict to keep the peace, you inevitably allow a compromise of your company culture. That's a failure of leadership that you don't want.

The misdirection strategy of avoidance is often expressed with phrases such as, "It's not worth my time" and "There are more important matters to see to." While there is credibility to the idea that priorities must be set, you should consider addressing that a conflict exists. Doing so will allow you and those you lead to plan for how and when it will be confronted. In my experience, misdirection is one of the most often used tactics of avoidance that leaders use to cover their fears of incompetency and rejection.

Suggestion: because you have direct influence on setting priorities, you can choose which conflicts to address first. If you have a greater fear of a certain priority, it's too easy for you to establish an alternate one.

To keep from falling into this trap, ask this question: "At this moment, what is the most critical conflict in my life?" Then create a plan to confront it. Begin with asking, "If this is the most important issue in my life, why am I avoiding it?" Then ask, "What is my first action to confront it?" You may notice I used the words "first action" rather than "first step." The latter can easily mean a "first step" to merely thinking about it. I am suggesting you plan to take action. You may want to add this practice to your daily to-do list. You will quickly notice that your effectiveness will increase dramatically.

/// *Over-accommodation* is a form of avoidance in which you find yourself giving in without opposition or disagreement. A close kin to peacekeeping, conceding to others and taking a submissive posture often masks the problems at hand. It also shows that you are afraid to stand up for yourself and for what you believe in. This false sense of compromise can result with both others and yourself questioning your commitment to your values. As we'll explore later in this book, there are times when accommodating another person's point of view or helping them to fulfill their desires can be productive. However, this is only true when it is employed toward a constructive solution.

Suggestion: there is a big difference between over-accommodating to avoid conflict and making a conscious agreement to create a mutual benefit. And there's a big difference between constructively responding to someone's needs versus being a serial people pleaser and winding up as a doormat. I often ask leaders that are over-accommodating to create a list of the relationships they are engaged in and explore the reciprocity and mutual benefit in each. This provides them with a framework to better understand their patterns of over-accommodation.

✎ *Positive procrastination* is thinking that if you wait long enough, the problem will go away. Sometimes, by some stroke of good fortune the conflict indeed does go away. In most instances, it disappears because someone has taken over the responsibility to deal with it. From time to time, we all have seen this form of avoidance pay off. However, the conflict has not really gone away; rather, it goes underground and becomes another elephant that everyone thinks should not be talked about.

Another popular form of positive procrastination that leaders use is commonly referred to as "a cooldown period." You ask yourself and the other party to break from the conflict, giving everyone an opportunity to settle down and come back to the conversation with a cooler head, clarity, and a better attitude. I am not advocating that you avoid this approach. In fact, it often pays great dividends. I have also observed leaders employing it at first and then failing to come back to the conversation later. Not only does this form of avoidance maintain the status quo, it can make things worse. The other party feels ignored and, rather than calming things down, the anger escalates.

Despite popular beliefs, you'll not always be aware you are procrastinating or doing it intentionally. I am certain that there have been times when you found yourself doing things that are more pleasant and fun, without intending to put off something less so. It's not always something you do consciously. There are also times when you have so much to do that procrastinating over unpleasant jobs—like confronting a conflict—seems normal, especially when faced with competing priorities. Something has to give. Unfortunately, the things that fall by the wayside are those that we don't like, yet need to get done.

Suggestion: this is the catch-all solution—when you see a conflict, confront it. Do it now. Step up, face the truth, and take action! If you add your conflicts to your "to-do" list, make sure they are at the top. Better yet, ask yourself why you need a reminder to do something that important. It's okay to procrastinate on getting what you want, but don't procrastinate doing what you need.

Not Accepting Responsibility

What these strategies and actions of avoidance all have in common is the lack of responsibility from the leader. If you find yourself either 1) employing one or more of the previous behaviors or 2) allowing someone else to employ one or more of these behaviors, you are undermining your leadership and lessening your influence, inviting dysfunction into your culture, doing a disservice to everyone that looks to you for leadership, and missing an opportunity to confront your fears and grow as a leader. You are also becoming a big elephant.

As a leader, when you avoid conflict, you are giving permission to everyone around you to do the same. By doing so, you feed the elephant and invite others to do so too. With time, your avoidance can easily become a fixture of the culture you lead. It doesn't take long for your avoidance to also affect your organization's performance. There are a number of reasons that this will happen. To begin with, because your avoidance of conflict is seen as a form of disengagement, others will also disconnect and detach themselves from the conflict and from their work. They can easily become cynical about what is happening and about your inability to confront issues. When skepticism appears, pessimism, sarcasm, and distrust are not far behind.

When distrust appears, one of the first things people do is withhold the truth. They become complaint to the unwritten rule of avoidance, leading to a lack of participation, problem solving, sharing of information, and taking risks. These behavioral patterns are all evidence that people are not taking responsibility. And why should they? After all, the leader is not taking responsibility. When you role model the behaviors of avoidance, you are giving everyone else permission to do the same.

Chapter Summary

✄ Broadening your definition of the word "confront" to recognizing its positive aspects will shift your thinking about what it means.

✄ The definition for confronting is "to face the truth."

✄ Rather than thinking of conflict as a form of separation, hostility, or combativeness, think of it as an invitation to a person you are in conflict with.

✄ Your role as a leader is to lead others to face the truth.

✄ By avoiding conflict, you'll find that you are taking the role of the biggest elephant.

✄ There are several forms of avoidance. None of them are aligned with great leadership.

✄ As a leader, when you avoid conflict, you are giving permission to everyone around you to do the same. It doesn't take long for your avoidance to also affect your organization's or team's performance.

Chapter 12

AIMING TO WIN

In the previous chapter, the focus was on avoidance and the consequences of not confronting or engaging in conflict situations. In this chapter, I am inviting you to explore an approach to confronting conflict with the aim of getting something you want. More often than not, leaders are looking to get some kind of gain and seeking an outcome that provides them with a sense of accomplishment and a feeling of self-satisfaction. It's part of their nature. One of the reasons you are in a position of leadership is that you find meeting a challenge and winning is naturally stimulating. Competition and achieving your desired outcome delivers a sense of joy, perhaps even ecstasy. The greater the odds you beat, the greater the feeling of elation.

As a leader, strong competition stirs an excitement within you. The stronger the adversary, the more fired up and determined you are likely to become. In fact, the joy of competing and winning can be intoxicating. The greater the risk and disappointment of losing, the more you may find yourself wanting to play. It is your nature to want to win. At times, you will find yourself in conflict simply to seek the next victory. Whatever you've accomplished, it just may not be good enough. Wanting more, you'll look for opportunities to compete further, at higher levels, and seek out or create conflicts that allow you to reach higher levels of self-satisfaction that contribute to your purpose, mission, or cause.

So what does winning look like? That depends on the relationship you're in and your desired goal. How you react to the conflict at hand will directly reflect the situation. What is the goal? What is at stake? Who is involved? What is the history of the relationship? What are the interests of others? What is the long vs. short-term gain? Who are your stakeholders? How will winning impact your future? When it comes to the possible outcomes, there are many questions that will arise and that you must answer.

The World Is Watching

One of the realities of leadership is that when you confront a conflict, others will be observing your actions. They will be curious about your motives and may make assumptions about them. Though this puts pressure on you, the notion that the world is watching can be a heady thought and will naturally feed your ego. It can also be a very scary thought. Even if your leadership role appears to be limited, you must accept the reality that your actions can have a much broader impact. In today's interconnected world, the potential span of your influence is much wider and deeper than ever. Therefore, you must also appreciate the importance of being clear about your personal definition of winning.

It has long been a practice of good leaders to pay attention to the expectations of key stakeholders in their lives. At the immediate level, these include your family and close friends. The next group is the people who matter a great deal to your success. Beginning with your coaches and mentors, this group includes the people that are primary to your growth and advancement; they contribute to how and what you receive as benefits and rewards.

If you are a Chief Executive, this group will likely include a Board of Directors, all the stakeholders of the company, and all investors expecting a return on your performance. If you a leader in a partnership or ESOP (Employee Stock Ownership Plan), they include all the owners that have a stake in the enterprise. They are all a part of your definition of success and winning.[1]

Depending on your position and role, your span of stakeholders can expand to include direct reports, business vendors, fellow team members, and customers. Needless to say, it is a good idea for you to think about and identify all the stakeholders that have an interest in your performance as a leader. By doing so, you will find that there is a larger number of people who are interested in how well you perform. The more significant the level and span of conflict you engage in, the more you'll find people paying attention to your actions. The higher the level of your leadership, the bigger the audience will be. The louder the accolades when you're doing well, the louder the criticism will be when you are not.

When it comes to managing a broader audience, there are a number of key elements that you will need to keep in mind to use and manage conflict successfully. For the greater the level of attention on you, the more aware you'll be of the consequences. The greater your awareness, the more you can refine and clarify a definition of winning that will serve you best. You'll also benefit from clearly understanding what the key outcomes are and how you need to achieve them.

The first of these is *an increase in the stakes* you are undertaking and trying to manage in each conflict. Though you already have a set of outcomes you are trying to achieve for yourself, you also have to pay keen attention to the additional results that others expect you to deliver for them. Your definition of success may not only broaden, it can also have multiple priorities that you will want to sort out. This is when you often realize that you can't be everything to everyone and you can't deliver everything they want or need.

When this happens, be honest about it. It's not hard to imagine or recognize that there is the potential for more conflict with those whose expectations you're unable to meet. Avoiding these will only get you more engrossed in situations and layers of conflict that you'll have to devote additional time and energy to. Therefore, in most cases, it will save you a great deal of time and effort, as well as the potential loss in your influence, to not procrastinate. I suggest getting out in front of them, confronting the concerns and conflicts in as timely a manner as you can.

An increase in complexity will inevitably present itself, challenging you to sort out the truths from the misconceptions, reality from assumptions, and to continuously look for the common threads in the information at hand. Find out what is important and separate it from what is unimportant. I am a strong advocate of the idea that complexity is the art of simplicity. In complex situations and conditions, the best approach is to begin with seeking and identifying the simple truths. They include the patterns and threads that help you to understand the relatively few issues and conflicts that give life to the multitude of situations you will encounter.

Understanding who is interested in what will help you manage the root causes and players in a conflict. It will be of value in strategizing and setting priorities on the more important outcomes, what issues need to be addressed, who to talk to, and the most effective forms of communication. When it comes to who to talk to, it will be helpful to identify the stakeholders who can give you the best insight and knowledge to better manage conflict.

An increase in urgency will appear, resulting in a need to act in a timely manner. I'm not telling you something that you don't already know. We all realize that things happen quickly. In any conflict there will likely be someone or a group of people that will demand timeliness or an immediate response from you. The longer they have to wait, the more they will feel ignored. Therefore, even if you don't have a good answer or solution at hand, letting them know you are aware of the situation and informing them about your next steps will be helpful in influencing and managing their emotional response.

An increase in consequences is a natural result of having a greater number of stakeholders and bystanders. It also comes with the roles of leadership that have increased responsibility including the number of people you are leading, the level and complexity of the strategy you are responsible for, and the importance and magnitude of the goals you are expected to achieve. It's a simple matter of numbers. In any case, the more challenging your role as a leader becomes, the more it will show up in what others expect and how they will respond. Because everyone will have their idea of what is a positive or poor result, they will inevitably find ways to identify consequences of your successes and failures. Furthermore, the larger the span of your influence, the greater the effect of your actions will be. Though you will never be able to identify everyone's concerns, it is a good idea to become as aware as you can of their existence and do your best to attend to them. Above all, expect that they will show up. If you are aware they are coming, you won't be surprised and you'll be more ready to respond.

An increase in emotional value will accompany every conflict. One of the challenges you'll encounter when you have a broader audience with wider expectations is that it becomes a more fertile ground for defensive behaviors. Sooner or later, the frequency of conflicts will increase. You will notice that people will build on the negative energy of one another and the levels of emotion, anger, and defensive behavior will rise. This may include blame, backstabbing, coalition building, intentional misinformation, and a host of other destructive and dysfunctional behaviors. It's difficult to manage it all, yet you have to start somewhere. Based on your priorities, you'll need to choose which require your immediate attention and how to confront them.

The loudest or most obvious source will not always be the one that will provide the greatest challenge. One of the things to look for as a leader is the withdrawal of an individual or group of stakeholders. Often, some will deal with increased feelings of dissatisfaction by retreating. It may be that they are afraid and their retreat is a form of avoidance. On the other hand, their withdrawal may be a strategy to gain your attention. If you are not responding to them, they may suddenly reappear into the picture with greater discontent and emotion.

Whether it appears as an increase in stakes, complexity, urgency, consequences, or emotions, it's important to be aware of the level of attention that you will be getting. Whether you are a leader of a small team or a multi-national firm, people will be scrutinizing how you manage the level of conflict you face. They will have their own definitions of winning and will want to know what your definition is. When it comes to how you manage and use conflict, knowing who the potential stakeholders are, being aware of their expectations, and astutely observing their behavior will benefit you tremendously.

Know Your Defenses

When it comes to winning a battle, it is often said that the best defense is having a good offense. In conflict management, you will likely find that your defenses will not serve you well; especially those that you use to your advantage to forcefully get what you want. In most disagreements and interpersonal conflicts, much like avoidance, aggressive and threatening behavior has limited value. In managing conflict, defensive behaviors can bring short-term success, but will most often result in diminished long-term influence and success. This is particularly true in business, where the conditions of mutual benefit and value are always in play. Often, when you use defensive behavior to get what you want, you'll find that others will eventually come to distrust you.

With time, as a result of defensive behavior, others will draw conclusions and assumptions about your intentions and motivations. This will greatly lessen the quality of their relationship with you. At best, they will be cautious with you. This is because your defensive behaviors will result in others seeing you as closed to feedback and unwilling to let go of your self-justifying and protective posturing. This will leave you at risk of being perceived as egotistical, closed-off, self-deceptive, and unwilling to be open to their views, perceptions, and criticism. You also risk giving an impression that you are disrespectful and uninterested in creating mutual benefit in your relationships.

When confronting and engaging in a conflict, winning can consume you to the point of not recognizing the unproductive patterns of behavior that you may be relying on to get your way. They are approaches and techniques that others will often recognize as overly competitive. They will see them as your need to appear superior and too interested in getting what you want. Needless to say, though you may get the sense that you are winning, the potential costs of permanently damaging your relationships typically will far outweigh a quick or temporary gain.

Knowing your defenses depends on being aware of the behaviors that you use to protect yourself from losing. These behaviors can be self-deceptive as much as they are unproductive in managing a conflict successfully. If you become aware of your defensive behaviors, you can trace them back to your emotions and further connect them to your self-concept. Unfortunately, if you are unable to recognize them, you will not gain the benefits of the power of choice. Here are a few of the more common defensive behaviors:

- Blaming others.
- Being over-critical of others.
- Humiliating people in front of others.
- Being belligerent and using abusive behavior.
- Shouting at people.
- Sabotage through the withholding of information.
- Forming coalitions.
- Being unresponsive and ignoring others.
- Using threats to maintain control.
- Never accepting "no" as an answer.

There are also subtle forms of defensive behaviors that are more difficult to be aware of, keeping you closed to someone else's information and point of view. I've observed that leaders can do this in a number of different ways, utilizing different behavioral approaches. Veiled questioning, covert challenging, indirect questioning, downplaying, and a lack of confrontation are all forms of defensive behavior that are subtle and can easily go unnoticed.

There is also a great benefit to gain when you realize you are falling into a defensive behavior. The first is you will realize that these defensive patterns will eventually fail you. With time, you will realize that your defenses, though they may appear to be your best friends, are not. Sooner or later they will interfere with your ability to use and manage conflict effectively. They will interfere with your success as a leader.

The more conscious you are with managing your defensive behaviors, the more you will understand the level of influence your behavior has on others. You will come to see that you are the chief steward of your culture. How you defend yourself will influence others to do the same. Your definition of winning will become the culture's definition. It's up to you to show everyone the constructive behaviors and positive paths to competing and winning. When you don't, you run the risk of undermining your culture. By sticking with your defenses and not changing your behavior, you'll be inviting a herd of defensive elephants into your culture. Beware, your herd of elephants will consume an excessive amount of time, resources, and energy, and will generate a mess that you will eventually need to clean up.

Chapter Summary

✎ When engaging in conflict as a leader, there's hardly a time in which you won't be trying to win.

✎ As a leader there's an excitement that gets stirred within when you are up against good competition. The stronger your adversary, the more fired up and determined you are likely to become.

✎ One of the realities of leadership is that when you confront a conflict, others will be observing your actions.

⫽ When managing a broader audience, you will notice an increase in the stakes, complexity, urgency, consequences, and emotional charge.

⫽ When it comes to how you manage and use conflict, knowing who the potential stakeholders are will benefit you tremendously.

⫽ Winning can consume you to the point of not recognizing the unproductive patterns of behavior you may be relying on.

⫽ The more conscious you become with managing your defensive behaviors, the more influence your behavior has on others.

Chapter 13

THE CONSCIOUSNESS TO CHOOSE

At some point, we all arrive at the moment in which we recognize our ability to choose who we wish to be. We begin to tap into our creativity, discovering new and better ways to meet our needs. When this happens, we begin to differentiate who we are from others. Based on what we want and how we get it, we begin to see ourselves as individuals. Soon thereafter, the first experiences of consciousness arrive and we learn to recognize our emotions. We discover what were once our hidden motives. The place we eventually arrive at is consciousness.

For each of us, our moment of self-discovery occurs when we are ready. Although we all travel the journey, we each take our own path. We are not all ready to become conscious at the same time in our lives; nor do we all reach the same levels of consciousness. This is what makes us all so unique. It is why self-actualization is much less a state than it is a constant and dynamic journey. You begin to discover what you are capable of and the joys of getting what you want, when you want it. That same consciousness allows you to judge and criticize yourself. For good or bad, you learn to connect what you do to what you get. You become aware of your choices.

There is an ancient Hebrew saying that states man was created for the sake of choice. We all enter the world the same way, including having the capacity of choice. Some will say that choice is a God-given gift; others will claim it to be a matter of personal responsibility. Regardless of your perspective, at some point in your life, you will recognize choice as the most powerful aspect of your behavior. Despite claims that our actions may not have been of our own doing, you also learn that no one can ever take the power of choice away from you. Regardless of the consequences, you get to decide.

Moving to Open Communication

In the previous two chapters, the focus was on the two more frequent approaches that leaders take in response to conflict—avoidance and winning. They are manifestations of fight or flight. We've become more and more sophisticated in how we use them, especially when we manifest them through higher levels of consciousness. At times, they can be useful. At other times, they are destructive, hold us back, and result in distrust. Eventually, when they are expressions of deep fear and defensiveness within your team and organization, they become the dysfunctions of your culture.

No doubt, you want to win. You want to win to be the most innovative, to achieve your mission, and realize your purpose. You want to compete in the marketplace and win the customer. You want to be more profitable and build your team or organization to deliver and fulfill its purpose and promise. It is how you do it that will matter most. Outwardly, you want to make sure that your organization and team have the best vision and strategy to win. You also need to get everyone aligned with the team's and organization's goals and definitions of success, including insuring that each individual can contribute to those same outcomes.

These are all critical aspects of your work that need to be accomplished to be successful as a leader. In order to achieve them, your team or organization has to develop two vital capabilities. The first is that its members must engage in healthy forms of competition. The second is that members of your team or organization must collaborate with one another and be team players.

At first glance, these two elements of success seem at odds with one another. This is because they are. To overcome this natural contradiction, we all make a commitment that we will work individually to contribute to the greater good of the group. This is the constant of great teamwork. It is also the definition of high performing relationships. As individuals, we will perform to our highest level and do so in contribution to the relationship. This integration of individual interest with group outcome will be one of your greatest challenges. This means that you'll need to openly confront and deal with the multitude of conflicts that naturally come with it.

Because it is so fraught with conflict, shying away from confronting and talking about the natural tension between individual competition and teamwork will not do you much good. And expecting to direct or demand everyone to forgo their own interest on behalf of group outcomes won't work either. Your ability to successfully manage it requires you to first and foremost always be open about it, discuss what it will look like, and set shared expectations for openness and exploration. This is an important insight. You will not achieve the level of cooperation needed to succeed without communicating openly and asking others to explore their own truth. This is likely not a new idea to you. You already know it to be true. That being said, your challenge is doing it consistently and well.

To engage your team and members of your organization in high-level problem solving and to work collaboratively toward your common goals relies on open communication. Here is an example of how quickly the evidence of this can surface.

I recently sat together with a group of leaders to discuss advances in leadership thinking. They were all quite experienced people that one would readily consider seasoned professionals. Among the dozen or so people around the large conference room table, several had served as CEOs of multiple organizations, including multi-national companies. The purpose of the meeting was to discuss best practices for facilitating groups of leaders. Most of the members of the group were trained in facilitation and teambuilding techniques.

It was easy to see that everyone wanted to engage and be included in the discussion. And it didn't take more than five or ten minutes for individuals to begin engaging in forms of informal competition. At first, members of the group talked to share their knowledge. As the meeting progressed, several began advocating their points of view. Aside from the person leading the meeting, rarely did someone ask a question or create a space for further inquiry.

At one point, as one of the members of the group was sharing an insight, another member challenged him and told him he was wrong. Away they went. It quickly turned into an argument. At first, they argued with leading questions. As it intensified, they stepped further into more direct discourse. "I disagree! Oh, come on!" one blurted out at the other. As the direct criticism of one another increased, so did their defenses: "I have as much experience as you do and I am telling you it can be done!" It was obvious that each thought they knew better than the other.

It didn't take long for others in the room to begin to feel uncomfortable. Eventually, a couple of people at the table took on the roles of the peacemakers, smoothing over the disagreement and tension that the two had created. The conflict was abruptly halted. The issue went unresolved and the rest of the group did not learn anything more about the topic at hand. The facilitator quickly pointed out that we didn't have the time to discuss it further and that we needed to get on to other items on the agenda. As a result, what was likely one of the most important issues that we could have pursued and learned from was not addressed. We had all participated in the subtle avoidance that prevailed.

At the end of the meeting, we talked about the takeaways each person gained from our time together. When we finished, one of the members reflected on the fact that all the issues that we talked about shared the same central theme. "It's all about communication, isn't it?" he asked in a leading manner. We said our pleasant goodbyes and each went on our way. The two members of the group that had engaged in the conflict congenially acknowledged one another and left. It's likely that each walked out of the room with the perception of having won the argument. Each was probably frustrated that it wasn't clear they did. I should note that the topic they had argued about was distrust.

What happened in the meeting is not at all unusual. You see it happening all the time. All too often, we see the opportunity that a significant conflict presents going by the wayside. The conflict goes unresolved and impacts the relationship of not just those directly involved, as well as other members of the group. We see this occur throughout our organizations, teams, and institutions. It is the result of the inability to explore the truth and create a shared understanding of the conflict. It establishes patterns of avoidance and the withholding of thoughts, observations, and ideas.

Of course, it is all about communication. Just like business is all about relationships. It always is. We readily claim it is conflict that gets in the way. This is an all too easy way out to take. It becomes the excuse and rationalization through which we avoid the real issue. Conflict that is actually created by the lack of being open and truthful about what is at the root of the issue. More often than not, it is our unwillingness to openly explore what is taking place in the relationships that gets in the way.

Choosing to Explore

To explore requires you to be open to the dynamics of relationships. In turn, it demands that you acknowledge and clearly articulate your own truth. It also means being open to the thoughts and ideas of others and listening to their truth. As a leader, you thus need to be conscious of your intention and align your behavior to it.

The question you will inevitably ask is, "How do I become more conscious and make the right choices?" The answer is as simple as it is powerful: openness. Being open to yourself, being honest with others, and listening to understand their truth is your key to success. To do this successfully will require a great deal of effort and practice on your part. You must not only confront conflict. You must also be constantly aware of your fears and other emotions so that you can choose the behaviors needed to succeed. Fortunately, conscious exploration is an ability that everyone has. That being said, the more you are aware of your ability and the more consciously you practice, the better at it you become. Conscious exploration allows you to connect your experience in the moment to your self-concept, including all the filters, assumptions, and perceptions that you have. It is being truthful with yourself and being open with those around you.

The result is influencing others with authenticity. You don't always have to have the right answer, know what needs to be done next, or have the perfect vision or strategy. When it comes to conflict, conscious exploration is being aware of what you are thinking, seeing, and feeling. If you have an assumption, being aware of it allows you to question and choose what to do with it. Rather than argue your perspective, you may choose to ask a question. Rather than avoid a situation because you are afraid of being wrong, you can admit to not having the right answer and ask others for their input. Choosing the path of communicating your concern is an invitation to others to do the same and engage in openness and collaboration. It is your path to creating shared expectations and to commit to a shared exploration.

Looking back at the events in the conference room that I discussed earlier, if someone had simply expressed that two of the members in the group had a disagreement, it may have shifted the moment to one of exploration. For that to have occurred, rather than smoothing over the situation, someone would have had to explore his or her own choice of behavior, choose to behave differently, and then confront the conflict. By doing so, it may have invited the remainder of the group to explore how to differently manage the situation thus changing the direction of the meeting. It may have also led to others being more open to exploring the core of the argument: distrust. The failure to face conflict comes at a high price, including the inability to solve problems and collaborate effectively. Collaboration, whether defined as teamwork, working in cooperation to solve problems, supporting one another, or acting in partnership and shared interest, requires a willingness to explore.

Turning the Pages to Part Three

In the first part of this book we explored the leader's unique relationship to conflict. The second part of the book focused on the leader's power of choice. This includes the journey of discovering your self-concept and how self-knowledge results in effectively confronting conflict and engaging in the exploration that leads to collaborative problem solving.

The third part of this book will provide you with the practical "how to" applications of your self-knowledge and choice, including a seven-step process for effectively using and managing conflict to achieve higher levels of success.

Chapter Summary

⫽ Two aspects of teamwork are critical to a team's success: members must engage in healthy forms of competition and they must work in collaboration with one another.

⫽ To explore requires you to be open to the dynamics of relationships and to listen.

⫽ Your ability to be open is your key to success.

⫽ Collaboration, whether defined as teamwork, cooperating to solve problems, supporting one another, or acting in partnership and shared interest, requires exploration on the part of those involved.

Part III

LEADING WITH INTENTION

Chapter 14

THE INVITATION

We have arrived at the point where we will put the various aspects of your unique relationship to conflict into practice and turn our attention to the strategic and tactical aspects of using and managing conflict to reach greater levels of success.

In my 25 years of experiences with coaching, working with, and developing leaders, I have discovered, studied, and experimented with a wide variety of models for managing conflict. The majority of these focus on communicating and advocating your position, sharing facts and the thinking behind them, asking the other party what they want, and finding a resolution. Many models similar to this approach will show you how to communicate your point of view and eventually reach a resolution.

There are also more direct models for conflict management that I found leaders using in which you state your dissatisfaction with a person's behavior and performance and agree that they will change it. Some include the final step of discussing the

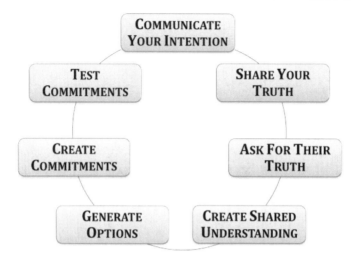

The Seven Elements of Leading With Intention.

consequences if either party does not keep their commitments. In light of the natural hierarchy in our relationships, the effect of the consequences will typically focus more on the person in the position of lesser power and influence.

The setback with most of these models is they do not create an exchange of thoughts and feelings that result in a shared understanding of the situation or relationship. They do not require a commitment to asking questions or listening to the other person's point of view. In light of this, the models that I found to be more effective include a step between sharing your facts and perspectives and identifying a possible resolution. They call for you to share your facts with the other party and then working together to define the problem and identify possible solutions.

With time, I discovered that most of the models aimed at resolving conflict were missing two elements of the conversation: intention and inquiry. These parts of the process are vital to building the mutual trust that is necessary to succeed. This experience eventually resulted in a model for confronting and managing conflict that requires placing intention at the beginning of the conversation.

Intention and inquiry are the invitations to the conversation. A conversation is the spoken exchange of thoughts that convey and connect us to our emotions. It is a dialogue that relies on our ability to be open to one another. It requires openly sharing what you think, see, and feel. A meaningful dialogue also necessitates listening openly to what the other party thinks, sees, and feels. As a leader, you must realize that every conflict, every confrontation, and every conversation has meaning. Each instance becomes part of your relationships with others.

Openly engaging in conversation, especially when facing the difficulties and fears of confronting a conflict, will define how others will assess their level of trust in your intention toward them.

Begin with Intention

When confronting a conflict, beginning with expressing what you want for the relationship is a powerful element in establishing the tone for the conversation. This also provides you and the other party with a shared picture of the type of relationship you are advocating. We all have intentions toward one another. At the interpersonal level, intention defines what you want the relationship to look like, including your longer-term goals for it. Exploring and thinking about your intentions toward others helps to define the essence of the relationship. It's likely that you will find yourself thinking about the mutual benefits and expectations that you have of one another.

At a deeper and more meaningful level, you will likely connect to emotional aspects, expressing your feelings about the level of trust, respect, openness, and honesty you expect from the relationship. Getting clear about your intentions toward others will provide you with a path to reaching the level of relationship you want.

When relationships become stressed or you are in conflict or disagreement with others, your intention toward them guides you in sharing your truth and hearing theirs. When you are conscious of your intention, you are better able to catch yourself when going astray from openness and trust. With respect to reaching a mutually benefitting resolution to the conflict, being clear of your intention provides you a compass to follow to find resolutions, reach new agreements, and make lasting commitments.

Intention is what we come back to and answers the questions, "What do I really want from this relationship?" and "In the end, what do I want and desire this relationship to look like?" As a leader, answering these questions provides insight into what you want from the conversation. It also reminds you that every conversation you have will be impacted by your intention for the relationship. As a leader, your intention toward others is how they will define your legacy.

When you are intentional in your conversations, you will discover that you are more aware of how you are expressing what you want to communicate. You are also more aware of how you are listening to the other party. After all, without listening it will be difficult to be intentional and fully open to the mutual benefit a relationship offers. And it's not likely that you'll understand what someone wants without listening to what they expect from you. This dynamic reminds us that to engage in a great conversation, we always have to listen and be curious enough to want to understand the other person.

There are typically two primary roles we take in conversations, the person speaking and the person listening. In each of these roles, you can take a more thoughtful approach and expand the conversation if you consciously move toward exploration. As the speaker, this means communicating what you are seeing, thinking, and feeling with greater awareness. As the listener, this means hearing what the other person is saying with greater interest and asking questions.

As the listener, you typically pay attention to what the other person is saying and interpret it in the manner that serves you best. Even as an active listener, when you ask questions, you can easily fall into surface listening and hearing only what you want to hear. Often, when you ask for more information and insight, you may use leading questions. In doing so, your active listening becomes a form of restrictive hearing and you wind up telling the other person what they ought to be doing or thinking. These unproductive and limited inquiries may sound like, "Have you thought about...?" or, "Have you tried...?" Leading questions are not the same as truly inquiring and listening.

When you act from a place of intention and move further into exploration, you are making a conscious effort to shift from surface level listening and telling, to asking the other person to share their truth, opinions, and insights with you. This higher level of inquiry requires you to engage in two primary behaviors of listening. The first is being silent and letting the other person speak. The second is asking questions that invite the other person to tell you more about what he or she is saying.

When you engage in exploration, you look for new insights and commonalities. Rather than just identifying differences, you seek to understand them. You focus on the words that others are using without criticism. You are being intentional in exploring what they are saying and interpreting their words in the way they are using them. You are hearing and exploring what they want you to know.

Mutual Respect, Trust, and Benefit

Leading with intention and your ability to beneficially and productively inquire will have a remarkable and positive impact on your leadership. This is due to the direct effects that intention and inquiry have on the level of mutual respect and trust they convey. This is especially true when you are in a conflict situation which, for you as a leader, is almost always. Once you focus on these elements, you will find that they also affect the other aspects of your communication with others.

It's extremely difficult to imagine that you can explore your intention toward others without exploring your own motivations. Furthermore, it's very difficult to be honest as to what you want and expect from a relationship without it. It is your own openness to sharing your thoughts and feelings, including your fears and concerns, that invite the other party to do the same.

Through intention and inquiry, you're not just inviting someone to a conversation; you are also inviting them to be honest with you. The more open you are to sharing what you think, see, and feel, the further you are inviting others to do the same. This is very powerful in building the mutual respect and trust needed to succeed in using and managing conflict.

What is the performance benefit of this? My simple definition for creativity and innovation is "the building of one idea on another." Communicating your intention and being inquisitive and open to listening to what others have to share are the tools and techniques that you use to leverage creativity and innovation. This has a great deal of significance and value in conflict situations. Through exploring and acting in alignment with your intention, and by inquiring and listening deeply, you are more likely to challenge your own thinking and come to better understand the underlying issues and causes of conflicts. Even in cases in which you are aiming to win, such as in a negotiation in which you are steadfast in your position, your ability to inquire and listen will help you determine what the other party's position is and how to best approach getting what you want. More significantly, if you're seeking to build mutual respect and find mutually benefitting resolutions, inquiry becomes an absolute necessity.

As a result, you are more likely to engage in constructive dialogue and collaboration. This allows you to engage others in discovering options and finding solutions that are more likely to meet the interests of all those involved. Further, it will create commitments that respond to the core issues and problems. In the end, this is the innovation and creativity you are looking for from others.

Through striving to understand and to respond to the core issues, you will often find that the lack of respect, trust, and openness are the actual hindrances. This is a reminder that by identifying and exploring them, you are moving toward finding a resolution that creates the mutual benefit you seek for everyone involved. The true test of an outcome or resolution to a conflict is whether it fulfills the intention for the relationship.

The Seven Elements

Intention and engaging in inquiry to clarify what others are thinking, seeing, and feeling are two of seven elements that make up the leading with intention model for confronting and managing conflict. My aim is not to lead you to believe that one or two of the seven are more important than the others. In the bigger picture, all of the elements are important and contribute to the success of the whole. As I mentioned earlier, the model is the result of my experience with several other approaches and frameworks to conflict management. My purpose in beginning with intention and inquiry is to focus on two aspects of communication that most leaders are challenged by. Even the most successful leaders I have had the opportunity to work with and who are clear about their vision and desired outcomes struggle with clearly defining and articulating their intention. They feel like they are not listening and inquiring well when dealing with conflict.

For these reasons, the seven-element model for leading with intention is the most effective framework that I have seen leaders using to reach the highest levels of success. It is as applicable as it is powerful, providing a framework that you can apply to just about any relationship in any part of your life. With time, you may find yourself adopting it as your approach to confronting and managing any conflict you encounter. You may also adapt it and eventually use it as your model for communication in all of your relationships, whether you are dealing with conflict or not.

In light of its application to any relationship, I encourage you to use the elements as parts of a step-by-step process. For example, in a highly emotional moment in which you find yourself under a verbal attack, you find it harmful to stop listening and begin arguing. In that moment, you may wish to explore and better understand the other person's point of view to find out what has them so upset. Using fearless exploration, you can take the opportunity to listen and inquire further to learn as much as you can. After collecting all the information and gaining the insight you need, you can respond by communicating your intention for the relationship.

Keeping in mind that the elements of leading with intention are yours to use in a manner that best serves you will give you additional flexibility in managing each conflict. Ultimately, it will reinforce your power to choose what to do and say in any moment and build your confidence. On the other hand, because it is a framework of elements, you can also apply it as a step-by-step process. Whether working with two people or with larger groups, you will find leading with intention to be a reliable and fruitful process.

Chapter Summary

- Intention + Inquiry = Invitation to the conversation.
- Openly engaging in conversation will define the level of trust that others will have in you.
- When confronting a conflict, expressing what you want for the relationship becomes a powerful element in establishing the tone for the conversation.
- Intention is what we come back to and answers the questions, "What do I really want from this relationship?" and "In the end, what do I want this relationship to look like?"
- When you act from a place of intention, you move further into exploration and consciously listen more.
- Leading with intention and your ability to beneficially and productively inquire will have a positive impact on your leadership.

⚏ Through intention and inquiry, you're not just inviting someone to a conversation; you are also inviting them to speak truthfully.

⚏ The model for leading with intention will challenge you to develop your own self-knowledge.

⚏ Leading with intention challenges you to be self-aware, conscious of your emotions, and use your power of choice wisely in what you say and do.

Chapter 15

CREATING SHARED UNDERSTANDING

One of the more frequent and challenging arguments in conflict is agreeing on what the truth is. When your truth differs from someone else's—situations that we all have found ourselves in—you can argue for some time as to who is right and who is wrong. Unless you agree that something is true under the same terms and conditions as someone else, you will continue to be in conflict.

Shared understanding is present when people are willing to understand one another's outlook, insight, opinion, analysis, observation, or assessment, and are considerate of one another's emotions. It doesn't mean that we have to agree with one another. This approach is of great value in confronting and managing conflicts: it is vital that you understand another person's wants and needs and that you are appreciative of their values. After all, what have you ever gained by opposing someone else's values? When you are open with others and are consciously inviting them to be open and honest, you are creating a means to clarity and insight as to why the conflict exists.

Creating a shared understanding is often difficult. To do so, you must invite others to actively explore one another's thinking and discover what you agree and disagree about. This requires you to openly express your thinking and reasoning and listen to understand theirs. To succeed, you must establish a level of trust with the other person or people involved in the conflict. There are four ways to inspire trust: 1) clearly communicate your intention; 2) share your thoughts and feelings; 3) invite others to share what they think, see, and feel; and 4) listen.

When you communicate your personal intention, you are being clear about what you want and need for the relationship and why it's important to you. You are advocating what you want the relationship to look like and how you want it to work. As a part of communicating your intention, you can also share, at the outset, what you'd like to achieve through the conversation and how you would like to see it unfold. Informing the other party how you'd like to see the conversation evolve will help them contribute to making it successful. It will also lessen the other party's fears, giving them a greater sense of confidence and predictability.

By communicating what you want the conversation to look like, you are also inviting greater openness. Being transparent to why and how you want to engage in the dialogue will initiate the level of trust needed for them to be truthful and contribute toward creating a shared understanding. Letting others know that you are interested in listening to what they think, see, and feel is an important aspect of finding the solutions to the conflict, including addressing the underlying issues. The ultimate goal will be to improve the relationship.

When working with a team or larger group, the same principles apply. Much like setting an agenda, identifying your outcome, being clear on how you would like the members of the team or group to communicate, and explaining the process will quickly improve your ability to manage it well. As with any group or team, establishing norms for how members are expected to communicate and listen to one another is best served by defining what a high-performing team member looks like, including these critical aspects of communication and teamwork.

When I work with teams, I often ask them to create a means through which they can look at the collective set of ideas and data, positioning it is an important step to creating a shared understanding. It not only contributes greatly to creative brainstorming, it also provides a platform for members of the group to be engaged and be heard. In the end, the process of creating shared understanding is often the single most significant factor to achieving the breakthroughs through which you attain higher levels of success.

Sharing Your Truth

To get really good at sharing your truth, it helps to be clear on its definition. Often, we confuse our truth with our honesty. It is important to differentiate between the two. Your truth is what you think, see, and feel. To understand your own truth is to also be aware of your self-concept, the perceptions you hold of others, and your judgments, assumptions, values, and beliefs. Your truth is your experience and, therefore, will be unique and different from the experiences that others have. This is particularly true in conflict situations.

Honesty is the behavioral expression of the level at which you feel safe to openly communicate your truth. Whereas arguing the truth can easily become an intellectual exercise focusing on facts, data, and sound reasoning, openness is also a reflection of how you feel. When you are being honest, you are not afraid of the effects of sharing your truth. When you are not being honest, you are fearful of the potential consequences of being open. Whether it's a fear of appearing incompetent, being wrong, getting ignored, being lessened in stature, or not being liked or accepted, your distress and fright will influence the level of openness that you will engage in.

In conflict situations, the bar of safety is raised, as is your emotional state. This makes it all the more difficult for you to be conscious of your choices of behavior and how open you will be. Though the span of openness runs from absolute and unbridled honesty to intentionally lying, there are multiple degrees to which we engage in being open. There are five choices of behavior that demonstrate your level of openness.

One choice you have is *lying*. When you are lying you are choosing to communicate something that you believe or know is untrue. Studies show that the majority of how people lie is not planned; it is improvisational and a response to an immediate fear they have. More often than not, you may hear yourself answer a question dishonestly and immediately wonder why you did it. We lie for any number of reasons. For leaders, it is typically due to the fear of feeling incompetent, embarrassed, humiliated and shamed, or not being liked. As we discovered in Part One, too often the leader's lies become the accepted lies and beliefs of an organization or team and establish dysfunctional norms.

The second choice is *withholding*. When you are withholding, you are sharing only part of your truth. A close kin to lying, the same fears and emotions will inform your choices. Unfortunately, though you may have someone else's best interest in mind and believe you're being helpful to them by not being direct or sharing only part of the truth, the recipient will more than likely tell you that what you're doing is the same as lying to them.

The third choice is *exaggeration*. Also often referred to as BS, it is overstating or stretching the truth. Withholding is sharing some but not all of the truth. BS is sharing the truth and then adding something to it. Although the same fears are at play, adding to the truth may lead to being more likable, appearing more competent, increasing your stature, or getting you more attention. Unfortunately, though you may lay claim to telling the truth and just stretching it a bit, others will call BS on you.

The next choice is openly telling the *truth*. As we have already defined truth and openness, I will only add that this is the most powerful form of communication. Though you may engage in one of the other three to gain or protect yourself from losing power and influence, your ability to choose to tell the truth is beyond reproach. It is worth repeating that, even in situations in which you are being blamed or criticized, the most effective form of leadership is being open and honest, and showing an unwavering willingness in telling the truth. Truth is an important ingredient in how people will judge your humility.

The fifth is *kidding*. I like to refer to this as the combo meal of communication. When you find yourself telling someone that you are kidding, you have very likely just lied. There are two ways that you can do this. In the first, you speak truthfully to someone and, based on your dissatisfaction or fear of their response, you then tell them that you are "just kidding." The other approach is to intentionally lie and then tell the truth by adding, "Just kidding." If you hear others kidding you often enough, it will likely leave you feeling insecure and unsure of their intentions and whether you can really trust them.

Though people use kidding to be playful or to build rapport with one another, too often it is used as an indirect way to communicate, especially when people are in conflict with one another. If you pay close attention, you will find the commonalities and consistencies in the kidding and trace them to a conflict you may need to confront. I often found that kidding is a way that cultures learn to deal with longstanding conflicts that no one has ever confronted and have come to accept as norms they believe will never change. In teams and organizations, it can easily become a problematic form of dysfunction, keeping people from engaging in open conversation about the issues that matter most.

If the kidding is aimed at you or about you, paying attention to it may allow you to gain valuable feedback and insight about how you are doing as the leader and about the quality of your relationships. Like anyone else, others may be delivering messages of disagreement or discontent, or use kidding as their own indirect way of letting you know that they have a conflict with you.

Moving to Fearless Exploration

When it comes to sharing your truth, one of the more powerful abilities to develop is to consciously shift from just acting or reacting to communicating in greater alignment with your thoughts and feelings. There are a host of natural barriers to being truthful, including fears that are heightened by conflict. Your choices of how open you will be are guided by balancing what you want with your fears about what you can't get or are at risk of losing. Your fears and concerns help to determine the level of trust in your relationships. They reinforce your past and current assumptions, interpretations, and stories that you bring into the present situation and relationship. The greater the level of fear and distrust, the more your behavior will be emotionally driven and automatic. As a result, you will tend to be more defensive, judgmental of others, mistrusting, and closed. You may also be more avoidant or overly accommodating.

By exploring and sharing your truth, you will realize when you are being defensive. As a result, you will be able to explore the fears and concerns that are making you act defensively. This not only allows you to articulate them, it increases your capability to take ownership of your thoughts, actions, and your role in the relationship. If you don't know what your role is, you must ask about it. Quite often, we work from the assumption that sooner or later we'll find out, guessing, or leaving the responsibility for others to tell us. If you are not clear about your role and contribution to the relationship, it is usually a good idea to ask. After all, how others perceive your role is the product of your influence as a leader.

When you communicate openly and honestly, you are role modeling mutual respect, thus inviting others to do the same. There is much to be said for sharing your truth and the power that you get from being intimate and vulnerable. You can't really expect others to be open to sharing their truth with you if you don't invite them to. There is no better invitation than you showing them how it's done.

Intimacy can be scary. After all, the more intimate you become, the more vulnerable you are. This is what makes the sharing of concerns and fears challenging. In your most intimate relationships, the true price of admission is your openness to share your own truth and that of others. And whereas being open reminds you of your fears, it is also the most powerful aspect of trust. As a leader, others want to know who you are and what your truth is. Telling your truth without withholding shows your willingness to be honest and authentic. It shows that you are always willing to explore and learn, and to be curious about the person you are. Your creativity and innovation is an outgrowth of your ability to explore your relationship to the world and the people in it.

Chapter Summary

- Shared understanding is present when people understand one another's outlook, insight, opinion, analysis, observation, or assessment and are considerate of one another's emotions.

- When engaging in a conversation centered on a conflict, there are four ways to inspire trust: 1) clearly communicate your intention; 2) share your thoughts and feelings; 3) invite others to share what they think, see, and feel; and 4) listen.

- To understand your truth is to also be aware of your self-concept, the perceptions you hold of others, and your judgments, assumptions, values, and beliefs.

- Your truth is your experience and, therefore, will be unique and different from the experiences that others have. This is particularly true in conflict situations.

- Honesty is the behavioral expression of the level at which you feel safe to openly communicate your truth.

- Whereas the span of openness runs from absolute and unbridled honesty to intentionally lying, there are multiple degrees to which we engage in being open.

- Your ability to explore and share your truth is a critical key to creating shared understanding.

Chapter 16

FEARLESS EXPLORATION

The next element and step in leading with intention, and a requirement to creating a shared understanding, is to listen and inquire to understand what others are thinking, seeing, and feeling. I call this "intentional inquiry," the act of inquiring and listening in alignment to your intention for the relationship. As a leader, you'll be reminded again and again of the importance of listening and its contribution to your effectiveness. In fact, it is key to being successful in just about anything you do as leader.

It is important to remember that, by definition, leadership is the art of influencing others to act. Because listening is one of the most potent forms of influence in human relationships, we can conclude that listening may be the most powerful source of interpersonal influence. We all want to be heard, understood, and to be shown respect. By respecting others, you show them that they truly matter. Of all the ways in which we influence one another, there's hardly any more powerful as listening. To experience being listened to in a way that leaves us feeling that we are truly being heard—that what we think, see, and feel is valued and understood—is incredibly powerful. It is the power of self-worth.

Ultimately, your ability to listen informs your self-concept. If you cannot listen and inquire for feedback and input from others, you will be uninformed about who you really are and, therefore, your choices are likely to be limited. You can too easily become rigid, trapped by your fear of what you will hear and learn about yourself. To listen at the level needed as a leader requires you to act fearlessly. I like to refer to this level of listening as fearless exploration.

Fearless exploration provides several immediate benefits. The first is the influence your openness has on others. By being open you invite others to also be open. Being vulnerable, authentic, and intimate are tantamount with being honest. When you are honest, you are not only inviting others to join you, you are also setting the stage for bringing your expectation for openness and honesty into the spoken realm. Although you can ask others to be honest, there is nothing more powerful than role modeling your own commitment to being open.

A second benefit is avoiding misinterpretations, misunderstandings, poor assumptions, and false conclusions. Having the ability to fearlessly explore allows you to ask yourself the important questions and bring them into the spoken realm. In doing so, you are not only testing your own thoughts, you are inviting and helping others to explore their own. In conflict, this becomes an effective way to question the origins of emotions and offers an authentic method to discover when you are thinking alike and differently. By doing so, you avoid pre-determined outcomes or premature and inaccurate conclusions.

A third immediate outcome is expecting the unexpected. No doubt, there have been numerous times in your life when you have been in conflict with someone and were holding onto a perception or assumption about him or her, or the situation. When you explore fearlessly you will learn to let go of the need for the predictability that feeds a need for control. At first you may find this to be unsettling. With time, unless you keep others from being honest, you will discover that not having control over what others say will provide you with the information and insight that you need. And though it may be that what you discover was completely unexpected, it is often the key to your success. Time and time again, I have had great leaders tell me about the significance of the unexpected, how it contributed to their success, and how they learned to be on the lookout for it.

A fourth immediate outcome is co-creation. Although the term co-creation is widely used by business leaders to describe management initiatives that aim at bringing together different people or groups to collaborate or jointly create a shared outcome of mutual benefit, or to describe an engaging customer experience, understanding its origins provide for much richer and deeper meaning. Co-creation has long been a facet of art including stage acting, improvisational and stand-up comedy, music, and artistic creation of all types providing rich forms of collaborative innovation.

Co-creation is a powerful way to think about how to collaborate, especially during conflict when energy is abound. Raw emotion is often a powerful form of openness. Although it may feel threatening when others express their true feelings and their emotions escalate, it is often then when they are best expressing their truth. In my experience, when two people get angry and escalate to the point of shouting, I often find that sitting back, listening intensely, and letting them vent is a great way to let them get their truth out. Anyone who has ever been in a good fight knows that there is a story behind it. When emotions run high, unless there is risk of physical harm, I suggest you sit back, go along for the ride, and listen for the story. In every conflict, you and the other party each have a role to play. You are both characters in the story.

When it comes right down to it, you have to work through the defensiveness and discover the truths that will enable you to cooperate with one another. The highest forms of collaboration take place when you and others are expressing thoughts and feelings without the fear of being ostracized, criticized, or rejected. When you find yourself in conflict, you are already acting from some level of defensiveness and fear, and are therefore that much more likely to have trouble recognizing and consciously moving past it. When you play fearlessly, you invite others to do the same. When everyone is being more open and expressing their truth, you drastically improve your probability of reaching a shared understanding and cooperating to solve problems and reach mutually benefitting solutions. To be a successful leader, you have to trust in yourself to let go.

Five Ways to Listen

When in conflict with someone, listening well is usually not easy. Yet, to be a great leader requires you to understand others, respect them for who they are, and pay attention to what they want to contribute. You must listen, ask questions, and then listen more. You must do this again and again, showing people that they are valued for who they are and what they have to offer. It's that powerful, it's that simple, and it's not easy.

When you are in conflict situations, it becomes that much harder to listen. For this reason, it's a good idea to look at the various ways that we listen to one another, especially how they apply to conflict situations. Because much like when we were young children, when we are not getting what we want or we are living with fear, we like to put our imaginary hands over our ears and not listen.

It is also worth acknowledging the technological changes in how we communicate and the profound influence this has on how we listen. We are more connected to one another than ever before. Yet too often we engage in one-way streams of communication rather than meaningful exchanges. We are quick to respond and tell others what we think and less interested in inquiring and listening. Because we pay attention to so many different forms of communication, we find ourselves not paying enough attention to what matters most.

For example, attempting a meaningful exchange of ideas through e-mail or texting is hardly a good substitute for a real conversation. You become distracted from your priorities, such as with the use of electronic devices during meetings and conversations when it is more important to be present and listening. I can't begin to tell you the number of times I ask my coaching clients if they have taken the time for face-to-face conversation. Rather than rely on one-way modes of communication such as e-mails and texting, I encourage them to take the initiative and role model how to engage in a dialogue.

By engaging in a direct conversation, asking questions, and fearless exploration, you will increase your influence and send the message that the person you're talking to is important. Without conveying this sense of significance, it is difficult to get to a place of true understanding and trust. To be a good listener you have to be diligent and practice—especially in conflict situations—lest you fall prey to diminishing your influence on others.

There are five archetypal ways in which we listen. They range from obligatory eye contact and nodding (while not really paying attention) to being fully present and listening so intently that you hardly say a word.

Distant Presence

Appearing to listen when you actually are not is known as distant presence. These moments are sometimes commonly described as "looking right at you and not hearing a thing." You may even be nodding your head in response to what is being said and making direct eye contact, but you're not hearing a word.

When engaged in distant presence, you are not really listening. The upside is that the moment you become aware of it, you can use this opportunity to explore why you checked out. Though boredom and impatience come to mind, you may be influenced by past experiences with the person thus distancing yourself from him or her. It may be evidence of an underlying resentment or lack of interest in the relationship, an indication that you have already judged the other party to be unworthy of your time. It may also be that you have felt ignored by others and, responding passive aggressively, you've decided to not listen to them.

FEARLESS EXPLORATION

Listening at the level of active and productive inquiry that encourages and invites the other party to openly share their truth with you, consciously seeking to understand what they are thinking and feeling.

TESTING TRANSLATION

Using questions and statements to assure you are hearing what someone is trying to communicate and testing your own interpretations and perceptions to better understand what the other party is telling you.

PERSUASIVE REBUTTAL

Listening to what the other person is saying to form your own opinion or disagreements, and waiting for them to finish speaking so you can tell them how things really are and what *you* want.

ARGUMENTATIVE REJECTION

Cutting the other person off when they are speaking and letting them know that you disagree and that you believe they are wrong.

DISTANT PRESENCE

The behavior that you engage in when someone is talking to you and you have the appearance of listening when you are actually not.

The Five Archetypal Levels of Listening

Distant presence can be employed as a form of avoidance. By not listening, you keep yourself safe from hearing about difficult issues, discourage questions to protect yourself, or be selective to what you want to hear thus keeping your position to get what you want. Discouraging feedback, engaging in unconscious accommodation, or using it as an unspoken way of safeguarding yourself can all be very subtle and unrecognizable forms of distant presence.

For reasons I am unsure of, leaders seem to have an increased propensity for engaging in distant presence than others. Perhaps it is because they like to be constantly active and stopping to listen doesn't feel right. Though I've worked with several clients who have been diagnosed with ADD or ADHD, I've met with many more who believe that they must have a form of it.[1] Whatever the reasons may be, they tell me that they often find themselves unable to stay focused for the length of time required to listen well. It may simply be that, because you have so much to think about and so many competing priorities and time pressures, listening well will always be a challenge. What you will find is that the more aware you are of distant presence, the better you will be able to change your behavior, giving the other party the attention they deserve.

Argumentative Rejection

Argumentative rejection includes behaviors such as cutting the other person off when they are speaking, verbally stepping on their words and talking over them, raising your voice and shouting at them, blaming, attacking, cursing, and of course, threatening them. These are just a few of the ways you can let someone know that you disagree with them and that you believe they are wrong.

I am not suggesting that you do not take a confident approach to sharing your thoughts and ideas. Being assertive can simply mean that you are sharing your truth with the other party and showing that you are interested in hearing their point of view. This differs from argumentative rejection where you only want to listen enough to aggressively fight back. Once you're at that level, you'll likely find yourself shutting the person out with the only aim of winning.

There are also a wide variety of non-verbal ways to reject what the other person is saying. They include putting your hand up and signaling that they need to stop talking, crossing your arms and shutting down, strongly shaking your head from side to side to say no, turning away, or even becoming physically violent. Or, you can get up and storm out of the room.

One of the potential consequences of argumentative rejection is that the other party disagrees and then withdraws. Very often, in teams, organizations, and relationships, this can easily result in passive-aggressive behavior. When someone tells you that they disagree with you and you respond with "enough is enough" or "live with it," you should not be surprised if they take a more passive-aggressive approach in dealing with you in future conflicts.

With distant presence, if you are in disagreement, the other person may walk away feeling that they've not been heard or they may feel heard even though they were not. As a result of argumentative rejection, however, they know very well that they have not been heard. You've made sure of it. They may leave the conversation angrier, disappointed, beaten up, or just decide to give up.

As with any of your behaviors, it's good to be aware of when this happens and be clear of the choices you are making. If you find yourself arguing a great deal, don't be surprised if people stop presenting you their problems, issues, and disagreements. When leaders frequently argue, blame, raise their voices, and behave in threatening ways, others will see it as a form of "shooting the messenger."

In some instances, teams and organizations will adopt argumentative rejection as a form of collaboration. That is, by challenging one another, its members continuously raise the bar, requiring one another to have a good argument. The message is if you can't engage in argument, you don't get a seat at the table. In such instances, it is important that everyone understands this to be the accepted way of doing things. Some teams have told me that it is their norm to argue over one another and to be combative. When this happens, it is easy to fall into defensive and rejecting arguments as people end up only listening to one another for the sake of arguing. For this method to have any chance of working, a position must be backed by facts, logic, sound reasoning, and must be understood by everyone. The reality, however, is that this requirement is quickly pushed aside by a leader who likes to be right all the time and who can easily take the lead by having the entire team argumentatively reject one another's thinking and ideas.

When you become aware that you or others are listening at this level, I suggest that you simply tell them. Sometimes being assertive to raise the awareness of others (especially in a team environment) by calling a time out isn't a bad idea. When you do call a time out, be conscious and clear about your purpose. Better yet, lead with intention for how you want the team to communicate going forward.

Keep in mind that using argumentative rejection virtually always has winning as the aim. More often than not, you will have little interest in what the other party may eventually get from the relationship, as long as you get your desires and needs met.

Persuasive Rebuttal

In my experience, leaders use this approach to listening the most. You know you're at it when you find yourself listening to what the other person or people are saying while forming your own opinion, holding on to your disagreements and oppositions, and waiting for them to finish so you can rebut. You have taken their words and ideas and neatly organized them for the purpose of telling them how things really are and what *you* want. You may have even used active listening skills to get the data that you need to convince others that you are right, get them to agree with you, and support your desired outcome.

There are several forms I see leaders frequently use to let others know they are wrong. A more subtle approach is through the use of leading questions. These are forms of unproductive inquiry in which you use questions to cloak your assertiveness, couching your arguments and statements as questions. This includes questions to get the upper hand by showing that you know more than they do thus allowing you to look good in front of others. You may also find yourself asking rhetorical questions allowing only you to answer or using inquiries that confirm your own ideas or ways to see things. Here are some examples:

"Have you tried...?"

"Don't you think that...?"

"How about you...?"

"Don't you agree that...?"

"Have you thought about...?"

"Why don't you try...?"

Add the word "but" to the beginning of each question and it makes it clear that you are saying "no." For example, "But have you tried...?" or "But don't you agree that...?" "But" is a refined way of saying "no." You are likely using it more than you think. Try to catch yourself saying "Yes, but..." It is a misleading and contradictory way of saying, "no." If you pay attention, you'll become conscious that you can use it to shape rebuttals that let you sound like you are in agreement with someone when you're really not. For example:

"I understand what you are saying, but..."

"I hear you, but..."

"That's a really good idea, but..."

"I agree with you, but..."

Begin a sentence with the word "but" and others will hear you saying "no." Yes, you are beginning to listen more than when you are in distant presence or argumentative rejection. And you are likely using what you are hearing to get your own point of view across to the other person, trying to get them to agree with you. Or, you can choose to use other fillers for "but" including "however," "yet," "nonetheless," or "except." Regardless of which you choose, the person or people you are saying it to will likely understand it as "no."

Using persuasive rebuttal prevents you from learning about the other party and keeps you from understanding their issues, including how important they are. In both the long and short term, it can hurt relationships and results in others fearful of not being heard or respected. It also perpetuates your own defensive behaviors.

When you are engaged in persuasive rebuttal, you risk being caught up in narrow-mindedness, your assumptions, and, ultimately, your fear of being wrong. Usually, when you are using persuasive rebuttal, you are not going to spend much time trying to understand the interests of the other party. When all is said and done, if winning is your only goal, you are listening merely in pursuit of your own fulfillment.

Testing Translation

Shifting away from persuasive rebuttal to testing translation and engaging in fearless exploration is likely one of your key ongoing communication challenges. As a leader, you like to solve problems and have answers. After all, these are the key reasons that you got to where you are. Unfortunately, they can also hold you back from becoming the great leader you want to be. Making the shift from refusing and rejecting what others are telling you to being open to hearing them is vital.

When you use questions and statements to make sure you're hearing what someone is trying to communicate, you are testing your own perceptions and filters. This will typically be the moment you are consciously shifting away from rebuttal and disagreement to better understanding what the other party is saying. When you test what you are hearing, you are confirming your interpretation and verifying the meaning and importance of what they are sharing with you and in the manner they intend. You are shifting from asking questions to demonstrating your position, to asking questions in order to make sure you understand theirs. To do this successfully requires you to be aware of your assumptions and predetermined ideas about the other party's intentions and motivations.

The most common approach to testing your translation is to openly share your interpretation and ask the other party if you are hearing what they want you to. "What I hear you saying is..." and "I'd like to make sure I'm understanding you correctly. I'm hearing..." are both very useful techniques. At times, you may have to confront your own fears of not being a good listener and let the other person know when you are struggling to understand their intention and perspective. Rather than blaming them for not clearly communicating, asking for help becomes a powerful way to let them know of your intention to truly hear them.

"I need your help. I want to be sure I understand what it is you want me to know" and "I am really interested in clearly understanding what you want me to hear" are examples of statements that invite the other party to provide you with what you need. Being consistent with sharing your own truth, you can also express your own fear: "I am concerned that I am not hearing and understanding you well enough. I want to share with you what I'm hearing and ask you to help me."

There are many advantages of testing your translations. For starters, you are improving your ability to listen while being conscious of your own thinking and actively testing it. This consciousness allows you to look for new insights and find how you may be thinking differently from the other person, as well as what you agree on. Often, because you are in conflict, you tend to listen only for disagreement and differences and you miss the opportunities to discover what you already are aligned with. When you do find differences, not only will you be able to confirm them, you can also work toward understanding them. Unless you understand the differences, it will be difficult to engage in collaborative problem solving.

Testing translation is often the first step toward fearless exploration. To engage in it successfully will require you to be aware of your own perceptions, fears, concerns, assumptions, and interpretations. When confronting conflict, by testing how you are listening to understand the other person, you are increasing your awareness and consciously developing your ability to invite others to be honest with you. You are also expressing your desire to be more open with them.

Fearless Exploration

If you think that being a fearless listener is hard, you are right. In fact, you will likely find it to be one of the most difficult and challenging undertakings of your life. You will also find it to be one of your most rewarding. To be a fearless listener requires you to be emotionally aware, conscious of your thoughts and feelings, and able to identify a desire or need which you fear not meeting. With fearless exploration you must recognize your fears, have the courage to confront them, and consciously choose the behavior necessary to overcome them.

Fearless exploration calls upon you to be conscious of how you are listening and whether you are acting in alignment with your intention for the relationship. It takes you from being a holder of your position to discovering the influence of your position on the relationship. When you are listening at the level of fearless exploration, you are engaged in active and productive inquiry that encourages and invites the other party to share their truth with you, allowing you to understand what they are thinking and feeling. Letting go of protecting your ego, you are more receptive and open to others. This includes not being triggered by their perceptions of you. Rather, you seek to understand their perceptions and their experience of your relationship. Deeper understanding, increasing mutual respect, finding areas of mutual benefit, and potential resolution and agreement are all possibilities that you are encouraging.

The difficulty comes from letting go of your ego enough to begin fearlessly listening to someone else's truth. Here are some examples of how to openly listen to the other person and asking them to tell you more:

"You said...I'm interested in hearing more."

"Tell me more about..."

"What else do you want to tell me?"

"What more do you want me to understand?"

"You said you're feeling disappointed. Tell me more."

"I'm very interested in hearing more about what you said."

"I am interested in knowing more. Keep going."

Often, the best option is to be silent and just let the other person speak. Your inquisitive look is all that is required. Using silence is difficult, however, especially when you feel impatient and have a sense of urgency.

Lastly, in contrast to using "but" in rejecting another person's truth, choosing to use "and" extends a powerful invitation. For example: "You said...and I'd like to hear more about what you are thinking." Through years of working with leaders, I have found that using silence and inquiring with "and" are powerful forms of fearless exploration.

"Yes, and?" is often all you need to be successful. Whether you use it as a question or as a means of communicating agreement and inviting innovation, it reminds us that when it comes to listening, the less we hear ourselves speaking, the better we're likely be listening. It is a simple and profound truth.

The Gifts of Fearless Exploration

To explore or listen fearlessly is an act of generosity. Because the essence of mutual respect resides in listening to one another, you are letting the other person know that you truly value them. When you openly listen to someone, you're being generous with your time. Along with love, time is one of the two most precious things we have in our lives. Listening fearlessly is thus an act of generosity. It is a gift to others as well as to your self.

When you are completely present to someone—that is, listening to understand what they are both feeling and saying—you are showing empathy and compassion. Empathy and compassion are not only gifts we give to one another, they are powerful forms of leadership influence. Though there are other ways to show empathy and compassion, including offering help and resources, none is more powerful than being present and listening to someone express their feelings. In general, leaders often fail to acknowledge how others are feeling and when they are struggling emotionally. You can easily overcome this failure by being present to the emotions of others.

Being intimate and vulnerable are not only traits of authentic leadership, they are also the best evidence of trust. Although sharing your truth and your deepest feelings are measures of your desire for openness and are invitations to others to be open, so is listening fearlessly. We often use terms such as "building relationships." This implies that we build trust, and through our vulnerability and openness, we create the intimacy necessary for our most trusting and loving relationships. I liken this to building a tower of wooden blocks. The taller the tower becomes, the more reluctant you are to add to it. You become increasingly afraid that if you add another block, the tower will come crashing down.

The same thinking applies to your relationships. You grow the relationship to the point where you are afraid of breaking it. By being honest and sharing your truth, you think the relationship will topple over and fall apart. This is the true fear of intimacy; it keeps you from openly expressing your own truth and fearlessly inviting and listening to the truth of others.

To overcome this fear and to be conscious of your choices, I suggest you consider shifting your intention from building relationships to unfolding them. Much like peeling away the layers of an onion, rather than fearing the truths in your relationships, work to unfold them—to open them up. When you engage in intimacy, you are continuously unfolding and exploring the truths of the relationship and, therefore, building trust. Should you then discover that the relationship is not working, at least you can be honest about it and decide how to best end it. Surely that's better than building it to a certain point and then avoiding the truth in fear of it falling apart. By doing that, you're likely find yourself in a relationship that isn't what you want it to be; one filled with resentment, anger, and disappointment.

Ultimately, fearless exploration is the biggest gift you give to yourself. By confronting and overcoming your fears and listening openly to others, you will also open up to the richness of feedback and knowledge that encourages and guides your learning, growth, and development as a leader.

In conflict, nothing will be more powerful than listening to others and gaining insight from their thoughts and feelings. And when you are challenged to face your own fears, remember that your path to creating shared understanding relies on creating trust and engaging in mutual reciprocity. This will give you the courage to engage others in creating the shared understanding that will best serve your leadership.

Chapter Summary

⚮ Through becoming emotionally mature, you realize that there are greater possibilities to achieving success. This has a profound effect on how you listen.

⚮ Fearless exploration is fearlessly asking others to share their truth and openly listening to them.

⚮ There is nothing more powerful than role modeling your own commitment to being open.

⚮ When you explore fearlessly, you will learn to let go of the need for predictability and control.

⚮ Co-creation is a powerful way to think about how to collaborate when in conflict, especially when you have a great deal of energy to work with.

⚮ Although it may feel threatening when others express their true feelings, it is often then when they are best expressing their truth.

⚮ There are five archetypal ways in which we listen: distant presence, argumentative rejection, persuasive rebuttal, testing translation, and fearless exploration.

⚮ There are many advantages of testing your translations, including looking for new insights.

⚮ Fearless exploration means being conscious of how you are listening and whether you are acting in alignment with your intention for the relationship.

⚮ When you are listening at the level of fearless exploration, you are engaged in active and productive inquiry. Often, the best option is to be silent and just let the other person speak.

⚮ To listen fearlessly is an act of generosity.

⚮ Being intimate and vulnerable are not only traits of authentic leadership, they are also the best evidence of trust.

Chapter 17

CREATING TESTED COMMITMENTS

The previous three chapters explored the first three elements of the model for leading with intention and how you can use them to create a shared understanding. A shared understanding is the result of how openly everyone shares their own truth: what each person or party thinks, sees, and feels. The greater the commitment to openness, the more you will understand another's outlook, insight, opinion, analysis, observation, and emotions. It is worth repeating how important it is to achieve a shared understanding of each party's wants and needs, and that you are thoughtful and open to one another, understanding what each person is seeking.

Creating shared understanding is an ongoing pursuit. Every time you think you've heard everything, that all the information has been shared and that you are aware of everyone's needs, don't be surprised to find that there's more to discuss. Remember to expect the unexpected. Be diligent in asking questions and listening to others. If anyone thinks that you are missing information, lacking clarity, or he/she believes they have not been heard, it is a signal to continue to inquire and listen. Because communication between people is ongoing and dynamic, always being aware will help you avoid your moments of impatience or other negative behaviors that impede your goals.

If you're coming up against resistance to creating shared understanding, it will be easy to blame the other person. The first step is to look at your own behavior and evaluate whether you are sharing your truth, inquiring, and listening well enough. There are multiple ways to assess how well you're doing: You can ask others for feedback. You can solicit questions. Continuing the dialogue is not about lengthening a conversation for its own sake; it's about gathering as much information and understanding as you need to collaboratively find solutions. From there, you can work toward reaching agreements and making commitments that lead to action.

In conflict situations among team members, creating a shared understanding will often be a key indicator of how successfully the team members engage in creating solutions.[1] Through the years, I have facilitated many strategic planning retreats and processes. As a result, I have engaged a good number of teams and partnerships to help them mediate and resolve their conflicts. One of the key observations from my body of work is that the heavy lifting is often not in creating solutions; rather, the real challenge is in getting everyone to share what they think, see, and feel, and then to engage at the level necessary to achieve shared understanding. As leader, it is difficult to overstate how much success depends on your influence.

Generate Options

Generating options in response to conflicts is where you will find the payoffs to the hard work of sharing your truth and inquiring into the truth of others. This is where innovation takes place and where creative energy emerges most. There are four characteristics that I find to be powerful sources of this energy.

The first is clarity on what you and the other party are trying to achieve. When you explore why a conflict exists, you will typically find a shared purpose and, thus, potential outcomes emerging. Having clarity of goals is evidence of your ability to collaborate to create mutual benefit and becomes a great anchor to generating possible solutions. This can often be just as powerful, if not more influential, than just focusing on the defined problem or issue.

The second is exploring how potential solutions satisfy your interests and needs, as well as those of others. Too often, options and solutions to conflicts fail to consider the desires and needs of those involved. As you look for solutions, you insist that focusing on the problem will supersede the personal side of the relationship and the conflict in it. In doing so, you ignore that which may matter most to you and others thus leaving the underlying and more important conflict unmanaged.

The third is that in the absence of fear, creativity and innovation abound. Though fear can be a great motivator, when it comes to freely expressing what you think, see, and feel, it quickly gets in the way. When there is trust and a clear definition of an intention for mutual benefit, we are usually motivated to think freely and express ourselves. Often, I observe people in conflict holding back their ideas. Because the relationship lacks trust, people withhold their ideas and refuse to take the risk necessary to find optimal options and solutions. Spending the time to communicate your intention and engage in creating a shared understanding will once again provide you with a payoff.

When it comes to generating options, the fourth characteristic is patience. Too often the sense of urgency gets in the way of creating a complete picture of your shared understanding. The same holds true for generating solutions. If you want to generate the options to find the best solution, don't let a heightened sense of urgency interfere. At this point, you've already discovered that being patient and fearlessly exploring each other's truth has provided you with fertile ground. It's not a bad idea to keep tilling and doing your best to get it right, rather than getting it fast.

This is not to say that timing is not important. When you become more proficient at using the leading with intention model, you will find that your conscious competency to use it will allow you to move faster. Even then, if you feel that you or the other party are not being open about disclosing your concerns or are seeking a quick fix, it's time to stop in order to identify and explore those issues. Not doing so will cost you more time and energy in the future.

It is always good to align your possible outcomes with your intention. It is your compass. If you find yourself going off course, then rely on your intention to bring you back on track. Depend on the qualities of the relationship that you developed through the process of sharing your truth, asking for and clarifying their truth, and the mutual trust established in creating your shared understanding. If this becomes a repetitive process, that's a good sign. It means that you are on the right track and learning to manage and use conflict more effectively.

It's also important to be flexible to the different styles of problem solving that you'll encounter. Along with differing personal preferences and personality types, you will also encounter a natural competitive nature that is likely already a factor in the conflict you're managing. Some people like to take an analytical approach with substantiation, proof, and data to seek verification. Others will want to take a participatory approach, looking for a high level of involvement from others. You may also find someone who wants to take a more freewheeling approach to unearth possibilities.

A good approach to dealing with these possible scenarios is to discuss how you'll do it before generating options. Much like describing the steps of the leading with intention model and inviting others to the conversation, talk about and provide a framework for how you will work together to find possible solutions to the conflict. This will remove some of the burden on you and convey your desire to work collaboratively, thus increasing the opportunity for success. At this point in the process, insecurities on how it will get done can easily take away from the trust that you've worked hard to establish. Once again, when things are not going the way you want them to, use your intention as the anchor to get back on track.

Making Commitments

The next step in the model is to explore all the options and possible solutions, and clearly articulate what each party will commit to doing. As I described earlier, spoken expectations become your commitments. One of the most common mistakes made at this point in the process is not openly talking about one another's expectations. Because you offered a solution, you may take for granted that the other person knows what you now expect. I suggest you always err on the side of clarity, specificity, and keeping commitments. The latter of these applies to everyone, including you. For that reason, the more you openly share your concerns and ask questions, the greater the level of trust and the better the likelihood that the promises you make to one another will be kept. There are several necessities to articulating and coming to agreement that will strengthen the commitments you make and contribute to how well they are kept.

- The commitments must be aligned with and clearly contribute to your intention for the relationship. Be in integrity with what you want for the relationship and who you want to be as a leader. Make sure that the only commitments being made are those that you and others are willing to keep.

- If there are measurable outcomes, state the commitments in a way that clearly defines the goals and contributes to their successful attainment. If you are going to reach higher levels of success, having measurements and clearly defined criteria is, in most cases, essential to accomplishing them. Clearly articulate and agree on descriptions and measurements including timelines, follow up, and any specific criteria that contributes to your individual and shared success.

⫻ Make sure that all measurable goals are attainable. I often find that, because you or the other person really wants the relationship to work, you end up trying so hard to please that it results in commitments that are not attainable or cannot be kept. Sometimes when a relationship shifts to greater levels of openness and trust, the parties involved get excited about the newfound ability to create mutual benefit. Though this certainly has its positive effects, it can also lead to overshooting what is realistically possible.

⫻ Your commitments must meet each party's interests and satisfy the emotional aspects of the conflict. Commitments that do not satisfy the shared need for mutual respect and benefit will almost always fail. If you do succeed, don't be surprised if it is temporary. If you don't work toward building trust for the long term, you'll get short-term results.

⫻ When making commitments, if you or others take a position of negotiation or compromise, bring your intention back into focus. When you are compromising, you are accepting that a fully mutually benefitting outcome is not possible. It is important that you acknowledge this and that you and the other party are aware and willing to make a commitment to compromise. Keep in mind that if you are agreeing to a compromise, you are likely to settle for less than what you really want. It's vital you are aware of this and are making a conscious choice. Typically, commitments that are compromises are evidence that a mutually benefitting solution has not yet been found and that the conflict is still unresolved.

⫻ It is important to discuss and commit to holding one another accountable. Talking in advance about the responsibility that each party has to openly communicate with one another when commitments are not being met is a key to successful performance. It's important to talk about and agree on the timeliness with which you expect one another to respond to unmet promises. If you don't, you shouldn't be surprised when someone avoids the new conflict that unmet expectations create.

⫽ Lastly, write the commitments down. Depending on the situation and who is involved, you may find it valuable to document the outcomes and, if need be, distribute them to those involved. It's useful to collectively draft an agreement, thus assuring that it is accurate and that all parties agree on its terms. Capturing your commitments in writing, or recording them in some other fashion, is best served when it is done with the intention to support and contribute to the success of the outcomes and the relationship. If you find that writing things down is perceived as a form of distrust, I suggest addressing those concerns. If you've come this far, you should be able to openly confront the issue and talk about it. If you don't, it may be worthwhile to explore how this informs and influences your thoughts and feelings about the relationship. That being the case, it's up to you to confront it. After all, as a leader, that is what you do.

It's Not About Compliance

When it comes to managing and finding solutions to conflict, it is important that you differentiate compliance from commitment. The difference between the two is quite significant. Compliance is a form of obedience. Compliant behavior is generally going to deliver only what is necessary. Typically, it is a signal that someone is not getting what they want. Not only might you wind up with forms of commitment that result in passivity from the other party, it can also result in a falling back to passive-aggressiveness and undetectable defiance on their part.

In light of the natural hierarchy that exists between leaders and their followers, and the layers of power within organizations and teams, solutions to conflicts can easily result in unspoken expectations of conformity and compliance. It is important to recognize this reality and challenge it when it happens.

As the leader, it is your responsibility to recognize when others are resolving conflict through the use of hierarchy and compliance rather than mutual benefit and commitment. I've worked with many leaders who insist that they have the final say, even when they allow their followers to make decisions. This is a signal to the people around them that it may best to figure out what the leader wants and use that to guide the agreements they make. This is especially true in conflict situations. When others use compliance as their guide to dealing with their conflicts with you, you miss out on the benefits of their thinking, creativity, and innovation. Eventually, you'll simply be unaware when others do have a disagreement with you. Acting out of compliance, they avoid confronting you. As a result, you may not become aware of it until it's too late. You will miss opportunities for leveraging the conflict to your advantage. Your team and organization will not benefit from it either.

Testing Commitments

Commitments are promises. When you make a promise, you give someone your word. As a leader, your word is your legacy. For this reason, I don't think I can ever overstate the significance and powerful influence you will gain from testing the commitments that you and others are making. When you test commitments, you are making sure that your words and actions are aligned with your intention of who you want to be as a leader.

By testing commitments, you are also assuring that your relationships with others fulfill your shared need for mutual respect and trust. This applies to each individual, regardless of whether your commitments directly impact him/her or not. As a leader, every commitment you make can easily take on a broader context, influence more people, and have much greater significance than may be at first evident. I can't overstate how much every commitment that you make matters. For this reason alone, it is critical that you test every outcome and commitment that you make.

The best approach to testing a commitment is when it is aligned with your intentions. Paying attention to the key attributes of a sound and meaningful commitment provides you with insights to what kind of questions you will want to ask; questions such as:

- Does it align to and support my intention for the relationship?
- Do the actions to be taken satisfy each person's interests and needs?
- Are each person's actions and responsibilities clearly understood?
- Are the risks and consequences well understood?
- Are everyone's timelines and measurements well understood and agreed on?
- Are the agreed upon individual and shared timelines and measurements attainable?
- Have we given one another permission to hold each another accountable?
- Are the consequences to breaking the commitment well understood and agreed upon by each party?
- Are the actions to the commitment documented accurately? Are they detailed enough to support the desired outcomes?
- Is there anything that needs to be talked about and that has not yet been discussed?
- Is everyone willing to keep their commitments?

The Final Test

When all is said and done, there are three questions that I suggest you ask yourself and that make up your final test:

1. Is it a commitment I am willing to keep?
2. Am I acting in alignment with my legacy?
3. What else do I need to do?

These questions are aimed at assuring that you are aligned with the core intention of who you are as leader.

When you begin applying leading with intention, you'll find that the best way of learning is to practice. If you are committed to applying the seven elements of leading with intention, you will eventually come to a set of conclusions about managing and using conflict that all great leaders understand.

- Managing conflict is not easy. It is demanding and requires a great deal of commitment and dedication on your part.
- Conflict is everywhere. As soon as you find yourself without a conflict to manage, you are not doing your job.
- There is hardly anything more rewarding than using and managing conflict to reach higher levels of performance.
- Each and every conversation matters. As leader, your influence touches many. Your words are your actions and every conversation is a dialogue of influence.
- You make mistakes. It's no secret that everyone does. The more important aspect is how you manage them.
- You are a lifelong learner. Every great leader is.

Chapter Summary

- A shared understanding is the result of how openly everyone shares their truth: what each person thinks, sees, and feels.
- Creating shared understanding is an ongoing pursuit. Every time you think you've heard everything or believe that all the information has been shared, don't be surprised to find that there's more to talk about.
- It is important to be flexible to the different styles of problem solving that you'll encounter.

⚉ Because you offered a solution, you may take for granted that the other person knows what you now expect. However, always err on the side of clarity.

⚉ There are several necessities to articulating and agreeing on what will strengthen the commitments you make and contribute to how well they are kept.

⚉ When it comes to managing and finding solutions to conflict, it is important that you differentiate compliance from commitment.

⚉ Commitments are promises. When you make a promise, you give someone your word. As a leader, your word is your legacy.

⚉ When you test the commitments that you are making, be sure they are are aligned with your intention.

⚉ Lastly, there are three questions to ask yourself and that make up your final test: Is it a commitment I am willing to keep? Am I acting in alignment with my legacy? What else do I need to do?

Going Forward:

CHALLENGING THE LEADERSHIP CRISIS

The world is turbulent, its waters roiled by scandals and a recent stock market crash. The political world is in upheaval, rocked by secret arms deals with terrorists and concessions to foreign despots who deal in drugs and have only contempt for the concept of human rights. The very fabric of our society is being unraveled by unchecked crime and drug traffic, increasing poverty and illiteracy, and unprecedented cynicism toward possible solutions. Who's in charge here? The answer seems to be, no one.

—Warren Bennis, 1989[1]

The time is now.

A quarter of a century has gone by since the late Warren Bennis wrote the book *Why Leaders Can't Lead*. I had just started the transition from being a chef and entrepreneur into my new career studying the psychology of leadership and the art of business and was immediately captivated by Bennis' work and writings. As a scholar of leadership, he was authentic and didn't withhold shar-ing his thoughts about the art of leadership. Nor did he reserve his ideas about society, business, and the human condition. By being honest with his views and opinions about the role and influence of leadership, he paved the way for the host of writers and thinkers willing to confront the challenges of leadership we face today. And though at times he could paint a grim picture, he could just as eas-ily be optimistic and hopeful about leadership and its influence on our future.

What I instantly saw in Bennis' work is an unwavering com-mitment to honestly expressing one's truth. Throughout his work, he painted a landscape of our business society that was clear, con-cise, and offered insights into the connection of the leadership to humanity and our shared pursuits in business and society that challenged leaders then, just as they do today. He was respectful, empathetic, and incredibly insightful. As a result, he was always guided by a remarkable capability to confront and define a shared reality with his readers.

In describing the complexity of the world at that time, Bennis offered a telling list of problems and challenges leaders faced in 1989. In this list he included: accelerating change; anemic or inept managers; the end of consensus in our society; big government; big media; big corporations; continuing hunger; crisis of public education; dehumanization; fragmentation of life; greed; corpo-rate gridlock; the hypocrisy of corporations; illiteracy; cover-ups; lobbyists; poverty; restrictions of freedom; further polarization of conservatism and liberalism; technology; Wall Street; and shifts in how we work.

Fast-forward to 2015 and we find that Bennis' list continues to paint an accurate and relevant picture. However, the inventory has grown. The list has expanded during the last 25 years and leaders today face new and more intense challenges. Among the problems and challenges we can add to today's list are:

Radical climate change.

The transparency of technology.

Global terrorism.

Social media and popularism.

Environmental crisis.

Healthcare.

Political gridlock.

Increased distrust of financial institutions.

Greater threat to personal freedom.

Eroding business ethics.

Hyper-connectivity.

Financial crisis.

Generational disconnection.

Global credit crisis.

Speed of information disbursement.

Increased scrutiny of character.

Privatized gain and socialization of loss.

The stakes are too high to ignore. Today's leaders are facing truly far more demanding and challenging problems than in the past. Needless to say, leaders have always been challenged with expectations of extraordinary performance. However, more than ever before, today's leaders are charged with providing the innovative and creative solutions that will lead others along new paths of exploration, discovery, and success. They are expected to inspire others to join them on the journey toward a more sustainable and better world.

Throughout my study of and work with leaders, I try to stay aware of the key questions that need to be answered: How will our leaders meet the challenges and demands of today's complex world? Is there a proven roadmap for them to follow in attaining success? Is there a formula for sustainable achievement? Which schools of leadership thought and philosophy are better than others? Is there one approach that outperforms them all? What truly lies at the core of great leadership and the character it takes to be a great leader?

The Elephant in the Boardroom is not intended to answer all these questions. The expectations we have of great leaders cover a broad span. My intention is to provide you with a glimpse into what we expect of great leaders, including how we expect them to face the challenges and problems of our time. My aim is to invite you to explore what lies at the core of great leadership and how you can manifest the trust, faith, and confidence of those that are willing to follow you. I offer what I hope is useful insight into how you too can show the courage, integrity, and capability required to be successful in today's complex, quickly changing, and turbulent world.

Although there is a greater demand placed on leaders today than at any other time in our history, I propose that it is within your power of personal choice and responsibility that you will find the courage to confront and overcome the fear that prevents you from facing these new challenges. This book is about you and is for you. To be an effective leader will require you to commit to the contribution you can make for the future of your world. Every leader will matter. You matter. Regardless of where you lead and who you lead, your influence and commitment to the future matters.

The time is now. It is calling you to contribute to the changes necessary to secure the positive future for the generations to follow. It is your responsibility to lead others in the creativity and innovation required to seize every conflict as an opportunity. If you are experienced, your call is to be a role model to the next generation of leaders. If you are young and a new leader, or aspire to become one, your call is to take responsibility for creating the future with those willing to follow you. Every conflict is a call to action that you must respond to. As a leader, it is your responsibility to act.

The world is yearning for greater trust in its leaders. From top to bottom and all across our organizations, communities, and businesses, there is a hunger for leaders with integrity and courage. I hope that through my work you will become more intimate with your unique relationship to conflict and how to build the trust that others look for. By becoming more intimate with your relationship to conflict and by developing the capabilities to more effectively and constructively manage life's conflicts, I believe you will succeed in learning how to be a leader and will accomplish the fulfillment you deserve. Rather than finding yourself in the role of the elephant, you will become the truly great leader you intend to be.

NOTES

Introduction

1. *The 2013 Executive Coaching Survey,* published by Stanford University and The Miles Group, provides valuable insight into the reasons that executives want and need coaching.

Chapter 3

1. As I describe in this part of the chapter, I often ask workshop attendees to look at conflict through the context of being engaged in competition. When asked if they now embrace it as competition, the answer I always get is a resounding "yes!"

Chapter 4

1. After the two popular fallacies of the sun rising and not taking things personally, the third most common

fallacy is "I can be nonjudgmental." The reality is that, at some level, we judge everything including ourselves.

Chapter 5

1. There are more elephants to spot than the 10 I include in my list. My goal is to list the 10 most valuable in my experience. I invite you to add to the list and tell me which elephant you find the most significant or presents you with the greatest challenge.

Chapter 6

1. For a complete list of the Culture Keys, I suggest reading Chapters 8 and 9 from *True Alignment*.

Chapter 7

1. There are six characteristics through which we can measure and observe teams and use as a framework for defining what an aligned and high performing team is: Focus on Results; Aligned Team Culture; Aligned Leadership; Open Communication and Conflict; High Performing Members; and Assessment and Improvement.

Chapter 8

1. I suggest it is an understatement to say that children will adapt easily to change. Change always has some form of fear attached to it. Even if you believe the change is in your best interest, you will still find that you have to let something go. You will almost always have to find a new way to succeed.

2. Laura Hillenbrand, *Unbroken: A World War II Story of Survival, Resilience, and Redemption* (New York, NY: Random House, 2014).

3. At the time of writing this chapter, my father Helmut had just celebrated his 84th birthday. On several occasions, death has knocked on his door. He has survived three open-heart surgeries, a coma, and numerous other

physical setbacks. Each day he rides his stationary bike for 45 minutes. He is a voracious reader and I often see the twinkle of a 13-year-old boy in his eyes. Each day he works to recover another piece of his dignity.

Chapter 9

1. It is said that the first 40 years of your life belong to your parents; the rest belongs to you.

2. The interview notes for Warren Buffet's definition of success are from Ivey Business School, Western University, Canada; (February 27, 2015); notes on the meeting that Dr. George Athanassakos and Ivey MBA and HBA students had with Mr. Warren Buffett.

Chapter 11

1. The Thomas-Killmann model is one of the more popular ones for understanding the different modes of conflict behavior. There are many other models and frameworks that provide similar approaches, descriptive modes of communication, and behavior. For further insight, I recommend reading "Relationship Between the Big Five Personality Factors and Conflict Management Styles" (*International Journal of Conflict Management*, Vol. 9, no. 4, pp. 336–355) by David Antonioni (University of Wisconsin, Madison).

Chapter 12

1. Here is a coaching process that is very useful and a great learning experience. First, make a list of all your stakeholders. Sort them into various categories such as family, friends, people you report to and who report to you, customers, suppliers, and so forth. Then prioritize them. For each category, make a list of what they expect of you and what you expect of them. You'll then quickly identify the causes of the conflicts you are engaged in.

Chapter 16

1. There is an ongoing debate as to the accurate level of diagnosis of attention deficit/hyperactivity disorder (ADHD). The current figures state that 5 to 11 percent of children in America, from 4 to 17-years-old, have been diagnosed with ADHD. There has also been much attention given to successful people with ADHD. Among them are Olympic swimmer Michael Phelps, comedian Jim Carrey, TV and radio host Glen Beck, actor Ryan Gosling, and inventor Dean Kamen. Others include: Richard Branson, Founder of Virgin; Paul Orfalea, Founder of Kinko's; and David Neeleman, Founder of Morris Air, JetBlue, and Azul Brazilian Airlines. When it comes to leaders with ADHD, evidence of the disorder generally focuses on issues related to planning and organizing, prioritizing, follow through, managing staff, and work-to-life balance. They also include consistency, focus, and self-monitoring. These last three provide the link to the behaviors associated with listening and one's ability to stay focused and mentally and emotionally present.

Chapter 17

1. As a coach, I always advocate the teaching of team conflict skills. As much as great leaders benefit from coaching, so do great teams.

Going Forward

1. Warren Bennis, *Why Leaders Can't Lead* (Jossey-Bass Publishers, 1990), pp. 114–115.

INDEX

ABOUT THE AUTHOR

Edgar Papke is a student and teacher of leadership, conflict, and the art of business. He is a globally recognized, award-winning speaker and author who is known for his authenticity and innovative approaches. He writes and speaks extensively about leadership and how leaders, teams, and organizations leverage conflict to achieve higher levels of performance. He is the author of *True Alignment*, which explores the human motivations of business and the alignment between the customer, brand intention, culture, and leadership.

Since 1989, Edgar has focused on the study of leadership, human motivation, and the natural role of conflict on our global business society. He coaches and consults with leaders and teams in a wide range of industries and institutions. Edgar delivers keynote speeches and lectures to audiences worldwide and was recognized as the 2013 Impact Speaker of the Year and 2006 International Speaker of the Year by Vistage, the world's largest CEO network.

Edgar holds a bachelor's degree in international business and a master's degree in organizational psychology from Regis University. He holds a culinary arts degree from the prestigious Culinary Institute of America and received its coveted Francis Roth Award. He has served as host for radio and public television and, as a singer-songwriter, has three albums to his credit. He resides and works in Louisville, Colorado.